Catch the Sparrow

Catch the Sparrow

A Search for a Sister and the Truth of Her Murder

Rachel Rear

BLOOMSBURY PUBLISHING
NEW YORK · LONDON · OXFORD · NEW DELHI · SYDNEY

BLOOMSBURY PUBLISHING
Bloomsbury Publishing Inc.
1385 Broadway, New York, NY 10018, USA

BLOOMSBURY, BLOOMSBURY PUBLISHING, and the Diana logo
are trademarks of Bloomsbury Publishing Plc

First published in the United States 2022

Although this is a work of nonfiction, the author has changed the names of
certain individuals to protect their privacy. Dialogue has been reconstructed to
the best of the author's or her interviewees' recollections.

Bloomsbury Publishing Plc does not have any control over, or responsibility for, any
third-party websites referred to or in this book. All internet addresses given in this
book were correct at the time of going to press. The author and publisher regret any
inconvenience caused if addresses have changed or sites have ceased to exist,
but can accept no responsibility for any such changes.

LIBRARY OF CONGRESS CATALOGING-IN-PUBLICATION DATA IS AVAILABLE

ISBN: HB: 978-1-63557-723-5; EBOOK: 978-1-63557-724-2

2 4 6 8 10 9 7 5 3 1

Typeset by Westchester Publishing Services
Printed and bound in the U.S.A.

To find out more about our authors and books visit www.bloomsbury.com and sign up
for our newsletters.

Bloomsbury books may be purchased for business or promotional use. For information
on bulk purchases please contact Macmillan Corporate and Premium Sales Department at
specialmarkets@macmillan.com.

Murderers are not monsters, they're men.
And that's the most frightening thing about them.

—ALICE SEBOLD, *THE LOVELY BONES*

AUTHOR'S NOTE

This book is the product of interviews, research, police reports, and newspaper articles. Events that involved me as a child, teenager, or young adult were drawn from memory.

The names of survivors of sexual assault have been changed, as have certain others to protect innocent people.

Events that are described were re-created from anecdotes shared with me by Stephanie's friends, teachers, students, coworkers, romantic partners, and acquaintances, as well as by police officers and attorneys involved in her case.

As much of this book relies on the memories of others, I am forever grateful for their generosity in sharing them.

PART I

Discovery

I

JUSTIN AND CHRIS had just started picking up speed on Justin's dirt bike, Chris balancing on the pegs, when the bike sputtered and stalled out. They were twelve years old in the spring of 1998, scrappy but both still a little short. Chris had brown hair and eyes, Justin blond hair and blue eyes, and mischief was often their goal. They were itching for speed, for action, for whatever freckle-faced boys yearn for on April afternoons.

That day the boys pushed the bike off the road near the intersection of Telegraph and Hurd, outside Holley, New York, a town that is home to one diner, one gas station, and an annual squirrel hunt dubbed the Hazzard County Squirrel Slam.

Past a hedgerow, the boys spotted a small stream. They loved to fish, so they couldn't believe their luck when they got closer to the shallow water and saw a flurry of foot-long fish in the water. "We've hit the jackpot!" said Justin.

The boys didn't have fishing poles, so they tried any other method possible—attempting to grab the fish with their hands, spear them with sticks, dam the water flow with twigs and rocks, and herd the fish as they moved in toward one another. Chris started chasing a big one downstream, wielding a stick—then stopped suddenly.

"Did you get him?" Justin called.

"C'mere," Chris whispered. "Just c'mere."

Justin made his way to where Chris stood, staring down at the water, and saw what had made him stop.

The stream where Stephanie's remains were found, 1998

Bones protruded from the water's surface, half submerged and half in the sun. The boys poked at them once or twice with sticks; they weren't bloody or fresh, just clean animal bones, and they'd seen scores of those. But soon they spotted something dome-shaped, with concave eye sockets and a few teeth.

A human skull.

★

THE BOYS GOT out of there fast. They knew the Hurds, whose farm it was, did not take kindly to trespassers.

"We can't tell anyone," Chris said, and Justin said, "Nope."

They ran back to the dirt bike, which thankfully started right up.

But that night, Justin couldn't shake the image of the skull in the water. As he ran himself a bath, he confessed to his older brother. "I swear it was real," he said. "It was a real human skull."

"Are you sure?" his brother said.

"I'm sure," he said.

As Justin lay in the bath soaking, thinking about the bones, his stepfather, Chad, knocked on the door and called in, "Is there something you need to tell me?"

While Justin pulled on a pair of jeans and a T-shirt instead of pajamas, Chris lay on the floor in the living room of his own house. The phone rang. His mom came and sat down close to him, and repeated the same question: "Do you want to tell me something?"

Justin and Chris sat in the back seat of Chad's car in silence, wondering if they were in trouble. Chad pulled over in a little clearing next to Bob Taylor's house, and the boys led him through the bushes to the creek. Chad aimed his flashlight where Justin and Chris pointed, doubting he'd see anything. The boys had probably got carried away.

But then his beam of light landed on the splotched skull with dark eye sockets. "My God," said Chad, "there it is."

They drove home to call the Orleans County sheriff, who came out right away to survey the scene. Soon the boys were herded back into the thicket for the third time that day.

Walking through the brush, the sheriff was on high alert. The late-night call was a shock; this rural county, sandwiched between Buffalo's Erie County and Rochester's Monroe County, didn't see much in the way of human remains, especially not discovered by preteen boys. The sheriff scanned the woods, his flashlight lingering on a couple of old beer cans. "Were you guys really out here trying to catch fish?" he asked.

The boys' eyes widened. They'd never had a sip of beer in their lives.

"It's right in there," Chad said, taking the attention off Justin and Chris to shine his light again on the skull in the water.

"We'll deal with you tomorrow," the sheriff said to the boys, then headed back to his car to radio for backup, and for the coroner.

★

THE POLICE HAD even more questions for Justin and Chris on Wednesday. They thought the boys had heard a rumor about a skeleton and gone looking for it. Justin and Chris maintained their account of the broken-down dirt bike and the gold mine of fish. And when a detective searching the area caught a "twelve-inch sucker" with his bare hands, they finally believed the boys.

Pathologists gathered all the remains they could find. They even collected several nearby birds' nests, which they hoped would contain some telltale scrap of fabric, anything that might help solve the mystery of who this was and what had happened. They compared the remaining upper teeth of the recovered skull—the lower jawbone was missing—to a set of dental records they'd had on file since 1991. By Wednesday evening, the police were able to say definitively what some of the cops were already suspecting.

It had been nearly seven years since the night she disappeared, on July 31, 1991. Now they knew where she'd been: decomposing in this shallow creek.

Finally police could deliver the report that hundreds of people had been waiting for all those years, including her immediate family down in her hometown of East Brunswick, New Jersey—my stepfather, Jerry, and my stepsister, Melanie.

It was her. It was Stephanie.

2

I WAS TWENTY WHEN my mother married Jerry Kupchynsky, and thus married into his family's mystery. A photo of my new stepsister Stephanie, who was then still missing, stood on the table with the wedding cake. It was the same photo as on the missing-person posters that had hung all over Monroe County for years. Stephanie's face at an angle, her wavy hair and sideswept bangs frosted auburn, a blush across her cheeks, her lips shiny with coral-colored gloss. Her eyes, large and brown as a Van Morrison song, gazing not at the camera but at someone out of frame, to the side, as if she were listening to the setup of a joke she wasn't yet sure was funny.

When Stephanie went missing from her apartment in Greece, New York, almost seven years earlier, she was twenty-seven; I was fourteen.

Her disappearance jolted the New Jersey town of East Brunswick, where we both grew up. Everyone knew the few facts about the case. A beloved violin teacher gone from the home she shared only with her pet birds. The sheets missing from her bed. Her checkbook found discarded on the side of the road. Her car abandoned in an airport parking lot.

That was all anyone knew—a beautiful woman was gone.

In the absence of any more facts, I spun stories in my mind. An illicit romance. An elopement. An escape to another life. An intruder, sweeping her off into the night. Alien abduction. Amnesia.

Her father, Jerry, the head of our school system's music department—a stoic man with an impenetrable Ukrainian accent—drifted hazily through my band class that fall. He had suffered from Parkinson's disease for longer than I knew him. His accent, paired with his head bobbings and arm wavings, inspired what my middle school friends and I thought were hilarious impersonations. "No su-it cases"—instrument cases, he meant—"in ze audience," he would say at concerts in the high school auditorium, standing five foot six at the podium. After Stephanie vanished, it wasn't funny anymore. He was even more hunched, more somber. As a younger orchestra director, he'd been famous for pulling devious pranks and bellowing at out-of-tune or off-beat instrumentalists. But he'd softened and stopped making jokes by the time I started high school. Dipping my head and casting my eyes in his direction, I told my friend, "He looks broken."

★

SITTING AT DINNER with my family in the weeks after Stephanie went missing, wiggling my feet in their black Converse All Stars under the table, I would ask, "How can someone be there one minute and not the next?" My parents hushed me with stern looks: *Don't scare your younger sisters*. But I was transfixed. Nothing like this had ever happened to anyone I knew. And Jerry awed me, forging forward day after day despite not knowing whether his daughter was still alive.

My own father—a loud, aggressive, six-foot-tall tough guy, Brooklyn born and bred—was nothing like Jerry. One morning when I was fourteen, just around the time of Stephanie's disappearance, my mother came to my bedroom in tears, holding a crumpled phone bill she'd dug from the trash. "Your father's having an affair," she told me. She asked me not to tell my younger sisters. Even then, I understood it was probably not his first.

Later that day, as I sat in our backyard, my father came out to talk to me. "Your mother says she told you about your father's affair," he said. "Well, your father wants you to know he's very sorry."

"Mm-hmm," I said.

Although he was a cruel man, abusive by any measure, it took me years to be able to use that word for my father's treatment of me. Yes, there were a few times I went to school with bruises on my arms where he'd punched me. He shook me violently when he was angry, and at least one of my friends called the Division of Youth and Family Services about him. Whenever I threatened to call, myself, he'd say, "Go ahead; they'll just come take you away from your family."

A neighbor of ours told me that one winter, when I was two years old, walking with my dad on the sidewalk, I wanted to walk on the unshoveled icy snow instead of the pavement. "You'll fall if you walk there," he warned, but I wouldn't stop. So he shoved me to make me fall on the ice.

"You'll learn to listen," he said.

Another time, when he walked me to the bus stop in first grade, I had to run home for my lunch box. As I ran back to the bus stop, I could see him leaning over and gesturing vehemently to an audience of laughing kids. My heart sank. I knew, even from a distance, that he was mocking me. "Your dad said you're so stupid you'd forget your head if it wasn't screwed on!" the kids jeered.

By the time I was in high school, he was reminding me daily how worthless I was, that I was useless, a "lazy good-for-nothing," that I would "never amount to anything," that no man would ever love me. It was constant, insidious. And there was his ever-present rage and yelling, his consistent hitting, punching, and kicking. Naturally feisty, I found it impossible not to fight back. When pushed, I bared my teeth and battled; maybe that's why my mother and sisters did not.

When I was sixteen, he punched me on the arm as hard as he would have punched an attacker, and the marks his knuckles made were visible for a week. He once kicked my sister Vanessa in the crotch so hard she couldn't walk; she was seven. Another time, my sister Laura hugged me after she'd emerged from surgery; she had numerous operations over the years on her ears. I hadn't wanted her to hug me, and I snapped at her. My father hit her for hugging me; she was twelve. But still I got the brunt of his attention. And honestly, the emotional and psychological abuse was much more intense for me than any physical violence, the pain of which was temporary and could be labeled clearly.

After my mother discovered my father's affair, his abuse of me intensified. I'd lost all respect for him after his pathetic attempt to apologize to me, and almost every dinner turned into a screaming match. My sisters, from whom I kept the secret, could not understand why I was always at odds with him. "Why can't you just keep quiet?" Laura would say, sitting with me at the top of the stairs while I cried. "You just make things worse for yourself."

When I left for college at seventeen, my father, lacking his usual target, focused all his cruelty on my younger sisters. But Laura was sixteen by then and wouldn't take it. "Go ahead," she once said to him. "Hit me! I'll kill you!" Another time, when he began shaking Vanessa, then twelve, my mother threw a glass at him, and it shattered against the wall.

My mother finally found the courage to leave him when I was nineteen. We moved with her into a small blue split-level house in another part of town. Jerry Kupchynsky, my old music teacher, was our next-door neighbor. His wife, Jean—Stephanie's mother—died the same fall, after a long struggle with multiple sclerosis. It was 1996. By that time it had been five years since Stephanie's disappearance; little had happened, and the case had stalled.

My mom befriended Jerry over the fence while they pruned tomatoes and pulled weeds together. Soon I received a quaint letter from Jerry in my college mailbox, asking for permission to date my mother. I was stunned; my father had never cared what I thought about anything he did, and Jerry was almost twenty years older than my mother. I thought they were just neighborly companions. But there was more there, much more. To me, he seemed gentle; he loved our dog Ben, and he expressed a desire to take care of my mother. Jerry felt like a better deal, like an upgrade from my father. He was gruff, but I trusted him. He was indomitable, but I thought I knew him, and I couldn't imagine him hurting anyone the way my father had hurt us. So I called Jerry from my dorm room to give my blessing.

★

THE TWO BOYS stumbled across Stephanie's bones seven months after the wedding. The medical examiner kept Stephanie's remains for testing, so it was another six months before we could have her funeral. I sat in the back row at the church on Route 18. That was when I first set eyes on Tom Redmond, the man my mother said Stephanie was going to marry. He sat between his two sisters in a pew near the front. An enormous portrait of Stephanie, half laughing at the whole ordeal, watched over my other stepsister Melanie as she played the Méditation from *Thaïs* on her violin.

Stephanie's ashes rested in a tiny box up at the front of the church, and were later buried at the foot of her mother's grave in Vincentown, New Jersey.

Jerry often said I looked like Stephanie, that when he stared into my eyes, he saw hers. It's true: my dark-brown eyes, almost too big for my face, are the same as hers. As Jerry's illness progressed into dementia, he often conflated Stephanie and me, as if seeking to resurrect her. One time, when I met him and my mother at Carnegie Hall, he grabbed her arm as I stepped into view. "It's Stephanie!" he gasped. A few years later, when he was in a nursing home, we visited him on Christmas Day, my birthday. My mother asked him, "Do you remember who has a Christmas birthday?" Jerry looked right at me. "Of course," he said warmly. "Stephanie."

Jerry died of Parkinson's disease in November 2009, his daughter's murder still unsolved. I sat by his deathbed with my mother for five days, where I thought I sensed Stephanie's presence on the other side of the worldly veil, waiting for her dad to join her.

She'd had a hold on me all that time. Why she haunted me wasn't clear. Was I seeking some ideal sisterhood, uncomplicated by the stains of abuse that mired my relationships with my own sisters in cycles of criticism and defensiveness? Did I think I could reach across death to procure that perfect sister? Did I think she was a kind of parallel me who'd fallen prey to some dark force I'd always known was out there? Did I think that if I could pinpoint how it happened, I could keep myself safe?

I'd started writing about Stephanie earlier in 2009, just months before my stepdad's death. But I wrote myself into an impasse; it all felt too heavy. I put it away and thought that meant I was over Stephanie; of course, I wasn't. I did not know that her case would be reopened in Greece the very same fall that Jerry died.

I turned away from Stephanie for six years, but still she called to me. Now, in 2015, I return to her. I contact Sandra Doorley, the district attorney of Monroe County, hoping she can help. "When will you be in Rochester?" she writes.

So I go, to try to unravel Stephanie's story, though I know it will end the same way: with her annihilation. Above all, it's some sort of reclamation and deliverance I think I crave, and maybe the truth will provide it—for Stephanie, my strange vanished double, my ghostly twin.

Y OU KIND OF look like her," Sandra Doorley says.
The Monroe County district attorney is perched on her enormous desk on a rain-chilled morning in June 2015, sporting a blond
ponytail and leopard-print skirt. Her office windows overlook
Rochester's copper statue of Mercury, with one arm stretched to the
sky. I've driven through five hours of downpour to start my journey
where Stephanie's ended.

I know from her emails that Sandra has not been able to let go of
Stephanie, either. "This is a story that needs to be told," she says. She has
hauled boxes full of binders and files from a storage room, and they sit
on a conference table waiting for me, like presents at a birthday party.

Sandra talks first about other stories that stick with her, cases she's
worked on as DA or, before that, ADA of Monroe County.

Michelle McMurray: raped, murdered, and tossed from a fire escape
at age seven in 1976 while her mother ran out for cigarettes. Found,
Sandra says, with "her panties pulled halfway up" and wearing "a little
Snoopy T-shirt." Michelle's murderer was not indicted until 2006.

Nature photographer Christine Sevilla: strangled by her husband,
whose "career was on the downfall," her body abandoned in a section of
a nearby park called Devil's Bathtub.

College freshman Alexandra Kogut, beaten to death in her dorm
room by an angry boyfriend, who used Alexandra's mundane
belongings—including a clothes iron—to kill her after an argument.

Her killer boyfriend claimed that the abuse he'd sustained from his father as a child predisposed him to murder. Sandra argued that he had a pattern of domestic violence and was guilty; the jury agreed with her, and he was sentenced to twenty-five to life. She describes to me the disaster he left in the dorm room. The kicker, she tells me, is that the school painted the walls and housed new students there the very next year. Sandra doesn't pull any punches. Her cheerleader looks and easy laugh cloak a tough and tenacious interior.

Sandra rifles through a box, then shows me photos of the shallow creek where Stephanie's remains were found. Little numbered placards mark the spots where various bones had drifted. Next she shows me photos of Stephanie's bones—those that had not been carried off by animals—displayed on a sterile coroner's slab, each bone in its correct place, a jigsaw puzzle missing a quarter of its pieces.

Around noon, a man with a booming voice whisks Sandra off to lunch, leaving me alone in her office for two more hours to explore the boxes' contents.

★

ONE THING I'VE learned about Rochester is that crime is common.

The night before, Dan, the bartender at the Owl House in the South Wedge—a hipstery, gentrifying neighborhood of Rochester—clued me in to the city's "Fatal Crescent," a coded, pejorative name for the intensely segregated, poverty-stricken five neighborhoods to the north of Rochester's downtown area.

In New York State, Rochester consistently has the highest murder rate, sometimes jockeying with nearby Buffalo. In 2015 it had a murder rate more than four times that of New York City. In fact, the only year since 2000 that New York City had a higher murder rate than Rochester was 2001, because of 9/11. In 2016 Rochester averaged twenty-one homicides per 100,000 people; the national average was five.

Mostly due to poverty in Rochester, in 2012 Monroe County had the highest rates of infant mortality in the state. In 2015 Rochester's own rocwiki.org stated that "Rochester has more people living at less than half the federal poverty level than any other American city of comparable size, with 16.2% of its people living in extreme poverty," and that "Rochester is the only mid-sized city in the country where slightly more than half its children live in poverty."

Kodak and Xerox, huge regional employers for decades, struggled to remain relevant around the turn of the century; they shed employees just as the Detroit auto industry had, destroying the livelihoods of many residents of Rochester and its surrounding towns. Together with Bausch & Lomb, they formed the Big Three of the area, at one point employing roughly 60 percent of the area's residents; now it's below 6 percent. Kodak alone had over 60,000 local workers on its payroll; by the end of 2016, this number had dropped to under 1,600. Virtually no comparable jobs could be found anywhere in the region. The depth of poverty since has been staggering, as well as the corresponding explosion of crime and murder, a great deal of it gang-related.

But still, something about Stephanie's murder struck a nerve with Rochester's jaded citizens. Bartender Dan remembers it. Shari and Nat, my Airbnb hosts, remember it—even that Stephanie was a much-loved music teacher. Sometimes I meet someone around my age who grew up in Monroe County, and they remember Stephanie, too. Sandra has clear visions of the posters hanging around town.

I force myself to think about this. Stephanie had the benefit of a family and friends who papered the city with her image. Also, Stephanie was beautiful, which wields a certain privilege of its own. And Stephanie was white; it's a fact I can't ignore.

PBS news anchor Gwen Ifill coined the term *missing white woman syndrome*, the tendency of American media to focus on these "damsels in distress." Eugene Robinson wrote in the *Washington Post* in 2005 that "the pattern of choosing only young, white, middle-class women for the full damsel treatment says a lot about a nation that likes to believe it has consigned race and class to irrelevance," suggesting that the disparities in media coverage merely reflect the prejudices of the consumers of that media. People's inherent biases paint certain victims as more innocent than others, creating both a racial and a gender hierarchy among the missing and murdered.

Black women are murdered at a rate three times that of white women. The 2018 murder of Nia Wilson helped bring into stark visibility the dearth of media coverage when black women are murdered. Because of the criticisms of the way Nia Wilson was portrayed by the media—for example, her local news station used a photo of her holding a cell phone as if it were a gun, painting her as a criminal and not a victim—her story became national news. Jordyne Blaise wrote in the *Atlantic* that "the story of her death has morphed into an allegory for the ways in which black people in America experience violence, sparking discussions about excessive use of force by police, media bias, America's history of racialized terror, white privilege, and black pain. When black folks, women especially, are killed in tragic ways, their families and communities rely on these discussions, critiques, and public pleas for them to be recognized, because the alternative is to risk not being seen at all."

Black women go missing at much higher rates, as well, but the media is four times less likely to report a missing black person than a missing white one. In Canada, a missing aboriginal woman is twenty-seven times less likely to be reported by the media than a missing white woman, a damsel in distress.

Think Laci Peterson, Chandra Levy, Natalee Holloway. White, middle-class, and attractive—just like Stephanie.

None of this changes the fact that Stephanie was my stepsister.

★

"TAKE THIS," SANDRA says when she returns, and gives me a gleaming CD. "It's everything."

Stephanie's case didn't develop much in the two years after her remains were found in 1998, and it went completely cold when the lead detective, David Connors, retired in 2000. When Greece police officers Stan Chizuk and Mike Ives picked up the cold case in 2009 after scandals left the ranks of the Greece Police Department in utter disarray, they scanned every piece of relevant paper onto a CD, the same one Sandra now hands over without a second thought. It's as though it's weighing her down, and she wants to be rid of it. She is passing the baton to me.

This is where it all truly begins—the moment Sandra hands me that shining CD.

★

ONE OF THOSE blazing-hot D.C. days, the kind that makes you remember you're south of the Mason-Dixon Line, I wake up in a little apartment around the corner from where my sister Laura lives with her husband and my two little nephews.

It's not long after my visit to Rochester, and I'm about to meet Stan Chizuk for the first time. He has retired from the Greece Police Department and is working on a naval base in D.C.

Lost for a moment in the underground tunnels of Crystal City, I emerge into a hotel lobby where Stan is waiting for me with his wife, Michelle, an effervescent woman with a bright Rochester accent who leaves us to go shopping.

The Rochester accent brings to mind the characters in *Fargo. Mary, merry*, and *marry* sound like the same word. *Rochester* becomes "Ratchesteh," and the open vowel *a* in *cat* is pressed into a diphthong, "kee-at." The accent can be charming, hospitable. But in a darker context, like recordings of Stan's partner Mike Ives interviewing criminals, there's something unsettling about the incongruity between those folksy, brassy vowels and the grisly subject matter.

I sit across from Stan Chizuk at the Holiday Inn bar. A bulldog of a man who chuckles and trips over words in his enthusiasm, he comes across as more of a gentle giant than a hard-nosed interrogator.

It is strange to be here when all the action happened almost four hundred miles north. But I start my voice recorder, feeling waves of impostor syndrome rise up in me; I'm no investigative journalist, just a woman with questions. Still, people keep feeding me every morsel of information they have.

I'm getting used to talking to cops; Stan is the third one I've met in three weeks. There's Dave Connors, who I met up in Rochester—the original head detective on Stephanie's case, from the time she vanished in 1991 until he retired in 2000—a cynic who suspects everyone, who ekes out details little by little, seemingly wanting to hoard them for himself. When I call him later with a question about some file on Sandra's CD, he says, "Wow, she really did give you everything, huh?"

There's Todd Baxter—the former Greece police chief who pushed to solve Stephanie's case after it was reopened in 2009, now the sheriff of Monroe County—a politician whose charisma disarms me. I find myself nodding along to everything he says when we meet for coffee. As much as I like him, I suspect he's sometimes performing.

And there's Stan Chizuk, who took over Stephanie's case in 2009. His amiability belies his sharp eye for detail. He seems to trust me, and he's the one who will become my true friend over time. He's a family man, a stereotypical-looking cop, and—unlike me—a Republican. (On a subsequent Independence Day, I'll send him a message saying "Happy 4th to my favorite Republican!" and he'll write back, "And my favorite Democrat: alcohol and fireworks don't mix.")

But at our first meeting in D.C. in the summer of 2015, that's all in the future, and I have no idea what to expect. Stan has a bag full of photocopied files for me, most of which I already have on Sandra's CD.

Like Sandra, he clearly remembers the missing-person posters plastered all over Monroe County in 1991, when he was a rookie cop in Canandaigua. The posters gave only Stephanie's height, weight, hair and eye color, and age—five foot four, 120 pounds, light brown, brown, twenty-seven—and the fact that as of August 1, 1991, she had been officially missing.

"There's an aftermath to your sister's death," Stan says. His choice of the word *sister* is one many other people will also make, even after I tell them Stephanie and I were not related by blood. Is it because they think I look like her? Is it because the drive and fascination I have for her story draw me somehow closer to her?

I ask Stan, too, why he thinks this case has worked its way into the minds of so many people, whether they'd met Stephanie or—like Stan and myself—had not.

"I'll be honest with you," he says. "This was a case you take personally. What her family was robbed of, what she was robbed of, was a terrible injustice. Her case deserves to be told. Your sister was a tremendous person. She loved her students; she was that teacher who would take her students out for ice cream. She was the girl next door."

I know what Stan means when he says "the girl next door"—a beaming, pretty girl who people said made the world a better place. But phrases like these are dangerous, I think. To assign a real person an archetypal identity is at best an oversimplification, at worst a form of dehumanization.

Maybe that's why, when Stan calls my stepsister "the girl next door," I feel my body tense.

"A beautiful young lady, the cold case part of it—this has what the American psyche likes. This is what they make movies about," former Greece police chief Todd Baxter says to me one day. He's right. I know this story. But again: this time, she's mine.

★

SINCE STEPHANIE'S DISAPPEARANCE, the descriptions all portray her the same way: a sunny girl with a bright future, sweet and beloved. Perhaps there's the occasional mention of her struggles—I've heard talk of how she stopped taking Prozac about a week before she vanished—but mostly she is vibrant, pure, and simple.

When I meet Stan in D.C., I still only know the barest facts of Stephanie's life: she was born and grew up in the same town I did, she went to college and became a music teacher—as I'd originally planned to do, too. She taught on Martha's Vineyard for two years, an experience that culminated in a deep depression. Then she moved to Greece, New York, taught for one more year, and met the man she planned to marry just months before she was murdered.

The files on Sandra's CDs will tell me a story that starts with Stephanie's death. But I want to go further back than that. So at the Vermont cabin where I cloister myself for three weeks after my trips to Rochester and D.C., I focus first on Stephanie herself.

I want to know her alive, in all her complexity. Who was the woman who moved through the world with a body around those bones? What was the mind inside that mottled brown skull? And what, if anything, placed her in the reach of someone evil enough to kill her?

I call her friends, her lovers, her teachers, her students. Only that way can I begin to know my "sister." Like me, none of them has been able to let Stephanie go. Like Sandra and Stan, they brim with information, anecdotes, testaments to how important Stephanie was to them. It's as though they've been sitting on the sidelines, waiting for someone to ask them to dance. Through their stories, I can almost experience things I never did: I can hear Stephanie's voice, touch her hand, laugh at her wacky jokes, smile because she smiles.

And yet there's one big difference. These people loved her when she was alive.

For hours and hours they talk to me; sometimes it's hard to get off the phone. All they want to do is talk about Stephanie, as if they can conjure her with repetition of her name. Her childhood best friend Jane says, "It's been so good to think of her, to skip over that terrible thing in my memory, to remember there was a Stephanie before that." That's the story they want to tell.

4

I T'S A LANDSLIDE!" the girl holding the ballot box on the auditorium stage said. "Her name is Stephanie Joy!"

Jerry Kupchynsky had agreed to let his high school orchestra students name his baby democratically, and this is how the baby girl born on February 17, 1964, came to be called Stephanie. Dark-haired and dark-eyed, she was the opposite of her red-haired and freckled sister Melanie, two years older.

She started playing the violin, as her sister had, at age five. Mediocrity was never an option in Jerry's house, though Stephanie was rambunctious and tougher to wrangle than the dutiful, docile Melanie.

Their playing, too, reflected their contrasting personalities: Melanie was more technical and keen, her instrument perfectly tuned and every note in place, while Stephanie was more reflective and soulful, playing with more emotion even if she also made more mistakes.

Still, by the time Stephanie reached sixth grade, she had surpassed every kid in her own grade. Her violin case was never closed, and her music stand was piled high with marked-up sheet music. She was always either just finishing practicing or just about to start.

Stephanie's mother, Jean, had been stricken with MS after she gave birth to Stephanie, and spent much of her daughters' childhoods being shuffled back and forth to hospitals. Jean was a talented pianist, but Jerry made her sign a strange contract stating she'd never interfere with the girls' lessons. Jerry wanted to be in complete control of the girls' musical education, and he didn't want his wife to contaminate whatever he accomplished. When Stephanie was eleven, Jean moved for good to a health-care facility, leaving Jerry to raise the girls.

He held the family together with a rigid authority and mediocre cooking. Stephanie often liked to escape to her best friend Jane's house, "borrowing" Jane's mother so she could feel, for an afternoon, a little more normal. At home she was constantly on the phone with Jane, stretching the spiral of the cord behind closed doors. Jane remembers hearing Jerry's voice, calling in his thick accent up the stairs from his studio, "Stephanie, are you practicing?"

Stephanie hated practicing. Then again, so did Itzhak Perlman.

In high school, she became more outgoing—and more ungovernable. Her room, once messy with dolls and toys, was now strewn with clothes, makeup, and albums. And Stephanie's friends all agree: she was a blast. Jerry didn't allow her as much freedom as other kids had, so she wasn't always combing through records at the mall after school or bowling at Carolier Lanes on Saturday nights. But when she was around, she pulsed and glowed.

Music blasted from her stereo as she practiced dance moves in front of the mirror in her bedroom, surrounded by posters of Pink Floyd and David Lee Roth. She had a way of pushing her tongue to the tip of her teeth when she laughed that reduced her friend Sharon Case to tears. She gushed over the "soooooo cute" gopher in *Caddyshack* after she saw it at Movie City 5. She hung around in the parking lot and in the hallways of the music wing at school, gabbing with her friends, always late for class. One fateful day in English class, her friend Michele heard a muffled humming coming from behind her, where Stephanie sat. Michele turned to find that an enormous purple wad of grape Bubble Yum had exploded onto Stephanie's face. Gum was everywhere: covering her eyes, stuck to her hair. Michele poked a finger through to Stephanie's mouth so she could breathe and hauled her off to the girls' bathroom. Their friend Holly followed them in to see what the commotion was. "Help me bring her back to life!" Michele said, and they giggled so hard pulling gum from Stephanie's eyelashes and bangs that they almost peed their pants.

Stephanie's sister, Melanie, loved to please her father. She was a peace-keeper, a role model, even something of a daddy's girl. She practiced violin without complaining, she looked after her little sister, she wore the cute dresses she was told to wear when she was trotted out to various public performances.

But it simply wasn't in Stephanie's nature to appease anyone. As with her violin playing, she had more passion and longing than she did precision and obedience. She rebelled against any confinements her father tried to impose.

Stephanie would wait until her father was asleep and climb out the laundry room window to meet her friends. She smoked, she drank, she blasted Van Halen. One rumor had it that she'd shown up to school one morning plastered on her dad's vodka.

Stephanie relished Marlboros and called them "Marlies" in a way that made it sound like the cigarettes were friends of hers. When she returned home after loitering by the 7-Eleven on the way from school, her dad would grab her coat collar and inhale, accusing, "You've been smoking!"

So Stephanie bought a bottle of cheap perfume to spray her clothes and hair. The final touch was one acrid spritz into her mouth. Stephanie never bothered to buy Tic Tacs or Dentyne. She had a kooky theory that the perfume worked better.

Stephanie was boy crazy. She dated an older high school dropout named Rich. They'd hang out after school, smoking and drinking beer. Rich was a brooding guy, quiet and tough. One night in his car her favorite Bruce Springsteen song, "Prove It All Night," came on. She started singing, and Rich, out of character, started singing along with her. Stephanie sang the same verse for weeks on end, flushing with girlish fervor, clinging to the rare moment of warmth she'd shared with him. "It was magic," she sighed to Jane.

She strove to be a normal suburban teenager, but her father, who'd survived Stalin's starvation of the Ukrainian people, being conscripted by the Nazis, and a displaced persons camp in Bavaria, was not a normal suburban dad. They were equally bullheaded, and their arguments escalated quickly because neither was willing to back down. Every fight was a continuation of the last one—one long struggle for control. Whenever

Jerry discovered some new transgression of Stephanie's, the neighbors could hear the two of them shouting.

One night, things got so heated at the Kupchynsky home that Stephanie fled to a nearby strip mall and called her friend Darlene, a young music teacher, on a pay phone. "I can't stand living with him anymore!" Stephanie cried. "Will you come pick me up? Can I come live with you?"

Stephanie sounded disconsolate, and Darlene said, "I'll come right now." But an angry, sputtering Ukrainian accent replaced Stephanie's voice. "Darlene, forget it! She is not coming to live with you; she is coming home with me. She will be where she belongs," Jerry said, and hung up.

When it came time for Stephanie to apply to college at the start of her senior year in 1981, she surprised her friend Michele by saying she wouldn't be going for music. "I'm sick of it," she said. "Violin, teaching other people violin, all of it."

"Does your dad know?" Michele asked, thinking there was no way this would fly.

"Yeah," Stephanie said. "He is not happy."

But her dad won. Stephanie eventually acquiesced and settled on music as her major, winning a scholarship to West Virginia University. Maybe college could temper her.

5

FINALLY FREE FROM the demands and competition of her father and sister, Stephanie soon realized she did like the violin, and she began to shine.

Stephanie's string quartet at WVU called itself the Cursed Quartet to honor their love of profanity. When they practiced together, any screwup would lead to a string of curses with which they soothed themselves after a missed note or a tricky bit of pizzicato. Stephanie often broke into obscenities in an overwrought Russian accent. "She sounded like Boris and Natasha from *Rocky and Bullwinkle*," says their cellist, Daniel, laughing. The group was close, and the other ensemble members, Valerie and Anne, all have their own funny stories.

Stephanie might have matured, but she hadn't grown much. She was only five foot four and about 110 pounds. Because Stephanie was such a tiny thing, and because sometimes she flapped her elbows like wings and tilted her head from side to side, imitating one, the quartet gave her the nickname Bird. Their rehearsals often devolved into parties; Stephanie made what Daniel calls "lethal" strawberry daiquiris, and she even invented a music-related drinking game, where the group would sight-read new arrangements, and if anyone made a mistake, they had to drink.

Stephanie started student teaching. "This is just for now," she told Valerie. "Until I make it into a symphony."

She practiced willingly, almost obsessively. She cried when she couldn't get it right and often struggled with her required piano class, flopping her head down on the keys and whining, "Why do I have to do this?"

It was a time of perfectionism. It seemed she was playing to an invisible jury, trying to prove herself even as Valerie would tell her, "I wish I was as good as you."

This perfectionism extended to her body too. She hated her hair and thought she weighed too much. Valerie and Stephanie went on a weight-loss crusade, eating nothing but bouillon and crackers and boring Anne and Daniel with their diet talk.

One summer, after going off to yet another music camp, Stephanie came back dejected. The teachers there had told her she was holding her violin wrong. The difference was tiny, but she worked to correct it, sitting rigidly in her chair, playing scales over and over. The quartet wanted to learn Ravel's String Quartet in F Major, but Stephanie was adamant she perfect her scales with her hands in the correct position before they moved on.

Sometimes Jerry would drive down on a weekend to pick Stephanie up. To Valerie, it seemed that even though things had been tough in high school between Jerry and Stephanie, their relationship now was fine.

Stephanie began dating a drummer, R. J. Vealey. He was her type, a rebel, but also a kind and courteous southern boy. He worshipped her, and tried his best to cater to her whims. "Aaaaaaaaarrrrrrrrrr-Jaaaayyyyy, I wanna gooooooo nowwwwww," she'd whine when she was tired, and they'd leave wherever they were.

One day Stephanie ran up to R. J.'s best friend, Dave Harrison, with a little sparrow cupped in her hands. It was hurt, and she begged him to take her to a vet with it. "Why do you give a shit about this bird?" he grumbled, but he'd seen how much she loved her parakeet Presto, so he drove her. She could be a real brat, Dave says, but she was gorgeous, with flawless skin and big doe eyes, and she was impossible not to adore. "She was a porcelain delicate flower with a screw loose," he says.

When she picked up a violin, tucked it under her chin, and raised her bow to hover above the strings, the members of her audience would collectively hold their breath. She was transformed. It was magic. Her musicianship was her trump card, but she lived in a cocoon of self-doubt, unable to see how she outshone the musicians around her, even as she snagged all the solos and won concerto competitions.

R. J. and Stephanie were together for almost three years before Stephanie broke up with him. R. J. was headed nowhere; he was smoking lots of pot and hadn't graduated yet. It was the end of the summer of 1986, and Stephanie, again following Melanie, who had graduated from there one year earlier, was bound for grad school at the New England Conservatory—and a life, she thought, of so much more.

6

"A BRIGHT STAR." SEVERAL people from the New England Conservatory use that exact phrase to describe the young Stephanie who arrived in Boston in the fall of 1987. There she made new friends, took up yoga, and was a brilliant student. Her energy and positivity in class were contagious, her hand shooting up in response to questions, other students often scrambling to write down what she said.

She drank and partied less. "I'm not gonna do that stuff anymore," she vowed to her new friend Jessica. Instead, she focused on her playing, learning from Carol Sykes (who had studied with Shinichi Suzuki himself) to teach in the Suzuki method. Carol recommended Stephanie as an interim teacher to a little girl on Martha's Vineyard named Meg Dole, and started driving her once a week to the ferry to the Vineyard to give private lessons. It was nearly a three-hour journey, but it was a good way to make extra cash and, more important, gain some experience as a violin teacher.

One of the first songs a Suzuki violin pupil plays is "Twinkle, Twinkle, Little Star." Stephanie would play both parts at once, fast, to make little Meg laugh. She could even play the song with her violin upside down.

Meg's mother Nancy was so impressed that when the Martha's Vineyard public schools were hiring a full-time strings teacher the next year, she urged Stephanie to apply. The timing was perfect; Stephanie was finishing up her master's degree in the spring of 1988 and didn't know what else to do. So when the opportunity presented itself, she could only accept. For her, it wasn't about the allure of the island; it was about the job itself. She would travel from school to school on the island, teaching new music students how to play violin, viola, cello, and bass, pulling them from their regular classes for small group lessons.

She arrived on the island with her pet birds, including her new cockatiel, Chubie, and moved into a small bungalow in Vineyard Haven. She started the school year in September 1988.

The students uniformly adored their pretty new teacher with the blue eye shadow. She stuck little frog stickers on the frogs of their bows, where the bowstrings are held together, so the kids would remember the name. She brought her cockatiel, Chubie, to school, training the bird to sit on her violin bow while she played. When teaching the students how to hold their bows properly, she instructed, "Make sure there's room to let Chubie through!" and placed her on their bows.

The students, from kindergarten to eighth grade, were delighted by the tickle of feathers under the curve of their fingers, always making sure to leave enough space for Chubie to fit.

Every Sunday Stephanie and her new friend Gail, an island fiddler and a fellow music teacher, ate brunch at the Black Dog Tavern. Stephanie had a wicked sweet tooth, Gail says; she'd plan on ordering an egg-white omelet but then often cave and get chocolate-chip pancakes instead. They were both the black sheep of their families, and both had sisters with superior performing skills. By this time, Stephanie's sister Melanie was playing with the Chicago Symphony Orchestra.

"We knew what we weren't," Gail says. "We were renegade property."

"The Suzuki method," she continues, "is based on the belief that every child is exceptional and worthy." Stephanie did not seem to believe this about herself. She had never really believed in her own inimitability. "She would have been lost under the iron rule of classical training," Gail says, but teaching—specifically teaching by the Suzuki method—opened her up.

Toward the end of Stephanie's first year there, Melanie came to the Vineyard with her new husband, a percussionist, to give a concert with Stephanie. The high school theater was packed; people stood in the back to hear them play Mozart, Schubert, Bach, and Copland. Between songs, Melanie and Stephanie charmed the audience with stories of their musical childhood, making light of being forced to perform when they weren't always willing. The audience laughed. Jerry, who had come up for his daughters' joint performance, was in the audience, laughing along with them. Things seemed to be going so well.

And yet Stephanie left the island the very next year. Jerry always said it was because she had seasonal depression. The Vineyard was "paradise in the summer but very depressing in the winter," he told the press after her disappearance. But by this point in my research, I know her a little better, and I sense there was more.

★

HOURS OF PHONE calls, emails, and meetings have gotten me somewhere I didn't intend to be. I wanted a more well-rounded Stephanie, and she's here with me now, less ethereal than before. I've tried my best to climb into the mind of a ghost, and I find myself thinking things like "She would have laughed at that," or "I can hear her saying that." She's almost reanimated within my imagination, and I wonder if that's what I've been after. I have begun to picture her facial expressions, though I never saw her face in person, hear her inflections, though her voice never hit my ears, assume I know what she would have thought, though we never met. She's become more than my muse now; she's my creation. I see her now when I look in the mirror.

And I know something else was up in Martha's Vineyard. Stephanie's leaving after just two years of teaching, when she was so well-liked by her students—something about it simply doesn't make sense. As ravenous as she was for authenticity, she was also devoted and shrewd. She was fiery, but when it came to her work—especially once she had discovered the freedom and self-actualizing power of the Suzuki method—she was deliberate. "She didn't need to disallow any of herself," her friend Gail says. "She was becoming the center of her own lotus flower."

Plus there were her students. One of them, Nina Violet, now a professional musician in her thirties, remembers Stephanie full of such love for the kids. At their end-of-year concert, after they had finished playing "Twinkle, Twinkle, Little Star," the first-year violin players sat cross-legged on the stage surrounding Stephanie and Meg, who stood at the center and played a Bartók duet. Nina was in awe.

Nancy Dole says Meg was really nervous and ended up playing the piece all out of order. "Wherever she was, Steph leapt to that spot and covered for her. Meg never knew, the audience never knew, only I knew," Nancy says. And after the concert, Stephanie hugged Meg tight and said, "We did such a great job!"

She would not have left those kids without an imperative reason.

I'm determined to understand what it was.

★

IN ONE SHORT newspaper article from the *Martha's Vineyard Times* after her case was reopened in 2009, an officer named Michael Gately said he knew Stephanie as a victim of domestic violence. I read and reread the phrase, remembering a fraught, violent romance of my own mid-twenties. I find a number for Michael Gately in the white pages, and call him up. The little bit he tells me on the phone is enough for me to know I have to go to Martha's Vineyard if I want to know the totality of what my stepsister experienced there.

I wait until the dead of January 2016 to make the third trip of my journey—Rochester, then D.C., and now Martha's Vineyard. I want to feel the full weight of a Vineyard winter. I stand outside on the ferry in the icy night. My hotel is mostly empty. In the morning, I find it's true what Jerry said about winter on the Vineyard. Everything's closed. The trees are bare. Some locals tell me that on any given summer day, there are over 150,000 people on the island. In the winter, that number withers to around 18,000.

The island becomes a skeleton between summers. The cold and isolation alone would be enough to give anyone a case of winter blues. But Stephanie had other reasons to flee.

7

THE FIRST TIME Officer Gately laid eyes on Stephanie, she was running down an ice-packed road, naked except for a pair of ankle socks that flashed like the white tail of a doe. It was around 4:00 A.M. and twenty degrees below zero. Martha's Vineyard was frozen and barren. Suddenly, as if out of a dream, a nude woman dashed across the beams of his headlights. Gately spun the car into a quick U-turn to catch up to her. She stopped running, wide-eyed in the headlight's beams. She was crying but docile. He took his police-issued parka and wrapped it around the terrified, trembling girl, coaxing her into the cruiser. "Show me where you live," he said.

Almost thirty years later, I am in the back seat of Gately's car, turning onto the same road where she directed him. Mud Puddle Path looks like a driveway, but behind the house visible from the main thoroughfare, the gravel track winds into the woods, and tucked away there is the small house Stephanie rented.

Gately, a shy, self-deprecating man, points to the window. In that house, on that frigid night in 1990, he tells me, sat Stephanie's boyfriend Geoff Fletcher.

Stephanie was playing in the orchestra for the Island Theatre Workshop when she first met Geoff, a talented pianist and composer. Like Stephanie, he'd learned he had an affinity for working with children. In August 1987 the *Martha's Vineyard Times* ran a story about him. "Only when you're willing to make yourself most vulnerable, only when you can trust the people around you, can you grow from the interaction," he said.

It was no wonder Stephanie fell for him. He was artistic, charismatic, with a strong personality. He referred to himself as "highly charged." He was fifteen years older than her.

The relationship turned problematic within months.

It was an alarming scene that winter night when Officer Gately returned Stephanie to her house. The booze on her breath was evident. Geoff was stoic and imposing. That's where Gately's memory gets blurry.

Gately didn't know what to do with this naked waif of a girl, who looked even tinier swimming in the parka that came down to her ankles. Was she safe back in her house with this man? He knew she was running from something, although he couldn't get the story out of either of them. "She was in fear of him, which was quite obvious," Gately tells me.

If he had arrested Geoff, as he thinks he did, there would be a record. But here I am on the island, and he can't find one. "Remember," he says, "you're dealing with the same courthouse that let Ted Kennedy get away with murder."

But Gately encountered Geoff again a few months after the night he found Stephanie, and that time he made sure to record every detail. The morning I leave the Vineyard, Gately hands me an envelope through my car window. "Call me after you read this," he says.

It's his report of that second encounter.

The report states that on May 7, 1990, Geoff called the police to report that "an inebriated woman had run away" from his home and was "suicidal." En route to the caller's home, Gately heard from the dispatcher: the woman was at her own home. He recognized Stephanie's address. He sped over. Stephanie was drunk again, in a frenzied state. Her legs and right middle and index fingers were bleeding. She "told me nobody cares about her and she would like to die," his report reads.

Gately tried to calm her, and he told her she should go to a hospital to have her wounds cleaned. He brought her to the Martha's Vineyard Hospital himself. From there, he called Geoff.

Geoff told Gately he and Stephanie had a "casual relationship" and had been drinking at a cast party. They left and went to Geoff's house, where Stephanie started coming on to him. When he refused her, Stephanie became irate. Geoff left to walk his dog. When he returned, she started arguing and removing her clothes. Geoff told her to put her clothes on and go home. She got dressed, then grabbed a shotgun from his wall, yelling, "You don't give a shit about me! No one does!"

Geoff said he grabbed the gun from her, and that's how she was cut. She ran out of his house, and he called the police to find her.

To Gately, the story didn't add up. He had a bad feeling about Geoff, and he'd now seen Stephanie twice under extreme stress after being in Geoff's presence.

"She could have been holding the barrel of the gun while Geoff was holding the business end," he says to me.

But in the end, there was no real crime. Gately had nothing to arrest Geoff for. He worried he hadn't done enough to help Stephanie, but ultimately he had to let it go.

Gately wasn't the only one who wondered whether Geoff was a threat to Stephanie's mental well-being, however. Stephanie's friend Nancy—little Meg Dole's mom—tells me a little about what went on between Geoff and Stephanie. Nancy thought Geoff was somewhat strange and had a big ego, but she also knew Stephanie could become unhinged and "wail, scream, carry on, and fight physically."

And Gail says the "relationship had a lot of sickness."

Years later, after Stephanie's disappearance, Geoff told the police she would throw herself against the wall and floor, threatening to kill herself. He claimed she would drive erratically when she was upset, that she liked to play the victim, that she wanted to die.

★

THIRTY YEARS LATER, Geoff Fletcher now resides in Florida. When I reach out to him, hoping to hear his take on the relationship, he responds by asking if he will be able to approve what I write about him. "My three-year relationship with Stephanie takes in a lot of time and experience," he adds. "It could take a few days. If we were to meet, would you come here?"

I write back to say it isn't feasible for me to travel to Florida, but I still hope to communicate; he replies that he will not be a part of my project.

Later correspondence adopts a legalistic tone. "Repeated entreaties from you constitute harassing behavior," he writes.

In the files Monroe County DA Sandra Doorley gave me, I learn that in the spring of 1990, Stephanie discovered she was pregnant, and in June she terminated her pregnancy.

Geoff later told the police he didn't realize what a strong effect the abortion would have on Stephanie. Stephanie's friends tell me she didn't want to end her pregnancy, but that Geoff convinced her to.

Sandra's files mention that the police were involved in at least two of Geoff's later romances, as well.

★

MORE THAN TWO decades later, during my winter visit, I contact the Edgartown District Court in Martha's Vineyard. The clerk there hands me a folder of all the public files she could find about Geoff. "You look just like your sister," she says. "I've had her photo on my desk since you called."

The folder contains a restraining order against Geoff from 1994, requested by the mother of his daughter, which was issued "without advance notice because the Court determined that there [was] a substantial likelihood of immediate danger of abuse." Geoff had sent her a seven-page litany listing all the reasons why he hated her, and the letter, which is in the folder too, made her fear for her safety. There's also an arrest record from 1997 for assault and battery against his wife at the time, who reported that he had broken her nose the year before, and who divorced him shortly after. Both women made sure to tell the police that he had a collection of firearms.

★

WHAT MADE STEPHANIE so desperate to leave Martha's Vineyard by the end of her second year there? Was it fear of Geoff and what he was capable of? Was staying in the place where she'd terminated a wanted pregnancy too much for her, driving past the clinic as she traveled from school to school too constant a reminder? Was her depression triggered by the lonely bleakness of the Vineyard off-season and worsened by her grief, or did the barren winter compound an already existent sadness?

Her relationship with Geoff is the darkest thing I've uncovered yet of her life. He unnerves me with his vague legal threats—I wonder if he still has all those guns. What did he say to convince her to have that abortion?

Michael Gately thinks Martha's Vineyard itself is cursed. "I've seen too many dreams crashed," he tells me. "Marriages blown up. Jobs lost. Suicides. Families destroyed." When he heard in 1991 of Stephanie's disappearance, Gately assumed that Geoff was involved. Up until Gately's retirement in spring 2016, the jacket he wrapped around Stephanie's shivering body remained in his locker.

Whatever it was, Stephanie was so desperate that she took the first job offered, in Greece, New York. It was there, one year later, that Stephanie would be murdered.

8

Discover the promise" is the motto of Greece, New York, a medium-sized suburb adjoining Rochester. On my trip to Rochester in 2015, I make the drive over past strip malls and sports bars, then park my car outside Stephanie's old apartment, watching birds on the electric wires. It's not the kind of place I imagine Stephanie, so quirky and creative, would have alighted. But maybe she would have gone anywhere to get away from Martha's Vineyard just then.

Through Kim and Carl Fink, acquaintances of her father, Stephanie had learned in the summer of 1990 that the Greece Central School District was looking for music teachers. That summer, as she taught at her father's summer string conference in New Jersey, her old teacher Darlene prepped her for her interview.

Stephanie got the job, and in August, she and another new hire, Molly Redmond, signed contracts to teach music starting in September for modest salaries of $30,000. Stephanie found a place in the Newcastle apartment complex. The apartments were uniform and simple, but the complex was one block from Highway 390, the fastest way to work, and Stephanie dreaded driving. There was a small kitchen, a living room where she could keep Chubie and her two parakeets, and a bedroom with a window.

As in West Virginia, Boston, and Martha's Vineyard, Stephanie made friends fast. They are happy to share their stories with me.

She went to the gym with Molly Redmond, joking as she counted calories on the treadmill, "There goes one chocolate-chip cookie!"

She and Molly would hang out at Stephanie's apartment, where Stephanie would gush about her birds like they were her babies.

She met Paula deFranco at a wedding to which Kim Fink invited her. They became fast friends. They practiced dance moves in Paula's living room before a ladies' night out. Paula took Stephanie to the mall—Paula driving, as she often did, since Stephanie hated to—where she bought a form-fitting little black dress. She let Paula's friends do her hair and makeup. She put on a chunky gold necklace, sheer black pantyhose, and heels. Paula snapped a photo of Stephanie before they went out. "This is the first time I feel like a woman and not just a little girl," Stephanie told her.

She befriended Maxine Ellison, a freshly divorced mom whose kids—both students of Stephanie's—worshipped her. Maxine was a music teacher in Rochester, and she offered to find gigs for Stephanie in the area. They played a few musicals at Pittsford Musicals and Arcadia High School.

Although Stephanie was reticent about her personal life at first, her inhibitions fell away and she began to open up. On long walks on the shores of Lake Ontario with Paula, she talked about how hard things had been on Martha's Vineyard. She still seemed very much afraid of Geoff. Stephanie told Paula he'd often called her "worthless." She'd sometimes tumble into self-contempt, telling Paula she'd be better off dead. She talked about suicide a lot. "Or maybe I should get myself a gun and go kill him," she once said bitterly. And yet Paula noticed she picked up whenever Geoff called, and continued to call him herself.

Maxine noticed the same thing. Stephanie bonded with Maxine over their recent breakups. She told Maxine that Geoff had been the major reason she'd left Martha's Vineyard, along with the abortion.

Stephanie talked often about how many months old her baby would be, and then broke into tears. She was enraged at Geoff, and even more so at herself for allowing him to push her around. She could not forgive herself.

"Everything is all my fault," Stephanie declared on the lake's edge one day as Stephanie and Paula tossed pieces of bread to the ducks.

Paula had confided in Stephanie about her abusive father and rough childhood, and she said, "Stephanie, I know you think you're the reason you've experienced all this pain. Well, you know I've gone through a lot, too. Do you think it's my fault?"

"Of course it's not," Stephanie said.

"Then why is it your fault, but it's not mine? What makes me special?"

Stephanie was quiet. Paula thought maybe, just maybe, in that moment, something inside Stephanie quickened. Soon Stephanie started seeing a therapist and taking Prozac to help with her bouts of depression. Her friends say she was starting to heal. "She started having the life she should have," Paula tells me. "She was blossoming."

And that spring of 1991, she decided she wasn't going to let anything stop her. She was ready to let love in.

9

"Look what I can do! I can make Chubie bounce! I can make Chubie dance!" Stephanie said to Molly Redmond's delighted music class. Stephanie and the band teacher had come to visit the students to show off the instruments they could learn the following year. Usually, strings were a harder sell than the loud, brassy trumpet or the pretty silver flute. But Stephanie was irresistible, playing her violin with Chubie perched right there on her bow, bobbing up and down in time to the music. The band teacher—who taught wind and percussion instruments—rolled his eyes at Molly. "I'll be lucky if I get any kids this year," he groaned.

Molly had a feeling her brother Tom would hit it off with Stephanie. Tom worked as a violin maker in Ithaca, so Molly convinced Stephanie to take her violin bow there to be restrung. Molly and Stephanie drove together one sunny Saturday morning in May, winding their way through the scenic Finger Lakes region. When they got to the shop, Molly introduced Stephanie and Tom, and though they were both quiet, she sensed their curiosity about one another. Molly didn't push; she let it unfold on its own.

Molly and her sister Dee had plans to visit Tom two weeks later, and Stephanie went along to pick up her bow. Dee felt a twinge of jealousy that her sister was bringing someone else for what she thought would be some quality sibling time, but as soon as she met Stephanie, Dee was charmed. When she saw Stephanie and Tom together at Tom's shop,

Dee saw the connection, too. Dee knew her brother well; he was captivated by this doe-eyed pixie of a girl.

Tom brought Stephanie's restrung bow over to her as Molly and Dee sat in the shop's burnished Victorian chairs. In his other hand, he held a violin he explained was an antique that cost $35,000. "Would you like to try out your bow on it?" Tom asked.

"Sure," said Stephanie, feigning nonchalance as she brought the violin to her shoulder. She launched into Suzuki's "Allegro," and Tom picked up a viola he had finished, its varnish dried to a glossy sheen. He joined in, and soon the two were grinning as they challenged each other with eye contact to play faster and faster. As soon as they played the last note, Tom began to play "Jesu, Joy of Man's Desiring," and Stephanie didn't miss a beat before catching on to the sonorous melody. At Stephanie's funeral, I heard Dee share her memory of the moment: "As I watched, a stranger to the musical art, I felt totally exposed, as if our bodies had at once been burned, and we were floating off in space somewhere. . . . As they stood there looking at each other, it occurred to me that there was actually light generating from them."

That night, the ladies went to watch Tom dance in a ballroom competition. Another friend tape-recorded Tom's jitterbug performance, panning out to the audience. Stephanie was caught on the video, a broad smile on her face.

From then on, it was understood Tom and Stephanie were an item. The next weekend, Tom came to see Stephanie in Greece for the first time. They walked along Charlotte Pier and had a romantic Italian dinner at Martone's restaurant. Tom spent that night at Molly's, but it would be the last night Tom and Stephanie were together that they didn't share a bed.

The 19th International Viola Congress was taking place at Ithaca College the following weekend, an annual conference to celebrate the viola and foster virtuosity of the instrument. Saturday morning, Stephanie got in her Nissan and drove to Ithaca to go with Tom. The weekend was a celebration of both their new love and their shared passion for string music.

They went to lectures and performances during the day, and a party that night. Stephanie wore red shoes, and some man called her Dorothy; she was tickled. Tom noticed all the guys looking at his girlfriend; he'd never had that experience before, of being the man with the most beautiful woman on his arm. That night, they sat together on the lawn outside the party. In the darkness, Tom's heart felt full. Stephanie was so cute, so lovable, so enchanting. The warm upstate night was filled with the peeping sounds of little frogs. Stephanie adored frogs; she told him she collected them. Tom knew then he was going to marry this capricious, guileless girl, so dynamic and alive.

The next weekend, school finally out for the summer, they headed to Martha's Vineyard to spend a few days with Nancy Dole and her daughter, Stephanie's former student Meg. On the way it rained a little, and Tom noticed that Stephanie's wiper blades were leaving streaks. "You really ought to replace those more often," he said, and she shot him a heated look, but didn't say a word. Tom took her cue and didn't say anything more. It was the only time either of them had offended the other, and it was over in an instant.

They took the ferry from Falmouth, a trip so familiar to Stephanie. Perhaps with Tom she felt strong enough to face returning to the place Geoff had nearly broken her spirit.

The weather was clear and sunny, but chilly enough in the evenings to wear long sleeves—a quintessential Martha's Vineyard June. It was while they were on the Vineyard that Stephanie confided in Tom that she'd been taking Prozac. She really was feeling better, though, and wanted to stop taking the antidepressants. She was scared to tell him, afraid of what he'd think of her. But Tom was nothing but reassuring. "Lots of people have chemical imbalances they need help with," he said.

Nancy was happy to meet the good man with whom Stephanie seemed enamored; it was clear he worshipped her. They returned to Ithaca on Tuesday, and Stephanie drove home on Wednesday. The next day, Tom came to stay at Stephanie's place in Greece. She was leaving soon for Ukraine with her father, her aunt, and her cousin Ivan to visit relatives. Ukraine was soon to declare itself independent, a harbinger of the dissolution of the Soviet Union, and with impending independence came relaxed travel restrictions. Jerry wanted to visit as soon as possible. Tom and Stephanie packed in as much time together as they could before she left on July 2.

She was gone for twelve days, to visit Jerry's cousin Milko and his wife, Marika, in a small rural town outside Strij. Milko had been educated by the Russians and was an undermanager for three collective farms, so he was fairly well off—by local standards, at least. Milko and Marika had a big house, but no running water. They had a cow, pigs, and chickens. Marika used almost their entire backyard to grow potatoes and string beans, because she could remember a time when they were under Russian rule and the Ukrainians starved. One night the whole family got sloshed on vodka, which is basically a requirement in Ukraine—they drank to togetherness, to friends and family, to their health, and to the proverbial horse that would know the way home no matter how drunk they got. "Budmo!" they said—a shortened version of a Russian phrase that means, "Let us live forever!"

Tom was as impatient as a high school boy waiting for Stephanie to come home. She returned on Sunday, July 14, but Tom had to work that whole week and had to wait to see her until the weekend. That same week, Stephanie stopped taking her Prozac.

Tom stayed with Stephanie from that Friday until Monday morning. They went to Abbott's for ice cream and walked along Charlotte Pier, admiring the lighthouse. They went to see the Rochester Philharmonic Orchestra and talked about the possibility of Stephanie moving to Ithaca. She was hesitant because she didn't have employment lined up there. Tom knew of one possible job, but Stephanie felt it didn't pay enough. Tom wanted to help her find a job that would satisfy her. He was going to ask her to marry him soon.

Stephanie still needed to earn a little extra money to make her rent. She'd sent a letter to her students' families, informing them that she was offering lessons over the summer from her apartment. "I find I really enjoy working with students in the more relaxed atmosphere that summer provides," she wrote.

After her first week of private lessons, Stephanie went to Ithaca for a visit; she and Tom spent a lot of time discussing the future that weekend. Tom felt courageous, despite the fact that they'd only been dating a month. The proposal burst out of him.

"Stephanie, will you marry me?"

"Oh, Tom," she said.

He was never sure if that was a yes or a no. Yet somehow he knew they would marry in time—he was certain of this, so he didn't pressure her by asking again. Their lives were already intertwined. Stephanie wanted him to come to New Jersey to work at her father's annual string camp. There was also a grand Kupchynsky reunion planned at her childhood home. Tom would meet Melanie and visit Stephanie's mother at her nursing home. He was nervous but excited to meet her family.

They spoke on the phone on Monday and Tuesday nights to iron out the details for the trip. Tom would leave after work on Friday to have dinner with Stephanie and her friend Maxine, and stay with Stephanie. Stephanie would leave for New Jersey Saturday morning, and Tom would join her after working Monday and Tuesday.

They didn't speak Wednesday, but on the night of Thursday, August 1, Tom called Stephanie four times, once after work and three more times between 9:00 and 10:30. She never picked up. Tom was worried, but told himself she had gone to bed early.

On Friday, Tom still hadn't heard back from Stephanie. There was a roiling in the pit of his stomach. He called her after work, then jumped in his car and rushed to Greece. He rang her doorbell; when she didn't answer, he felt faint. Stephanie's neighbor came out. Stephanie's car hadn't been there for a few days, her neighbor said, and she'd missed all of her lessons on Thursday and Friday. He showed Tom a note a student had left on the outside door. It had fallen down, and he'd taken it inside and stuck it to Stephanie's mailbox.

"Where are you?" the note said.

10

S TEPHANIE HAD A busy afternoon planned for Wednesday, July 31, 1991. After a slow morning at home, she had one violin student, a boy named Joshua, whom she taught from 1:30 to 2:15. She told Joshua they couldn't schedule any lessons until after she was back from her father's summer conference. She explained that she was bringing her talented student Heidi with her, and that Tom would join a few days later as the camp's resident instrument repairman.

After Joshua's lesson, Stephanie began preparations for her trip. She was a nervous driver, and Jerry had encouraged her to get her '85 Nissan Sentra checked out before the long drive. Stephanie made her way to the Jiffy Lube on East Ridge Road in Rochester, stopping first to browse at the Music Lovers Shoppe in Greece. She made a bank deposit and got to Jiffy Lube at around 4:00. When she left about a half hour later, she went to AAA to pick up a TripTik—a printout of complete directions from her apartment to the conference—so she'd feel more confident on the drive to New Jersey.

That evening Stephanie dressed in a summery white tank top, blue-and-white flowered shorts, and white Esprit sneakers to visit her friend Maxine. With Maxine's children, they took a drive to Abbott's Frozen Custard in Ontario Beach Park. It was a verdant upstate day, the sky clear and the temperature mild. As they walked on the boardwalk with their ice cream cones, Stephanie was in high spirits. Swinging a brown Esprit purse by the strap as she spoke, she told Maxine that she was excited to have Tom meet her family, and that she was planning on interviewing for a job in Ithaca. She grumbled a bit because a janitor in her apartment complex told her she shouldn't be giving violin lessons from home. "Well, I'll just move to Ithaca!" she said, shrugging it off and giggling.

When she left Maxine's place at 9:50, she said she needed to stop by the grocery store on her way home. She made a quick trip to the Tops market and got home a little after 10:00. At 10:16, she called her father and left an upbeat message. "You must be teaching. The car's ready, and I have my TripTik. Could you double-check the roads? I'm looking forward to seeing you!"

And then she vanished.

PART II

Disappearance

MISSING

5'4" Tall
120 lbs.
Light Brown Hair
Brown Eyes
Age 27

STEPHANIE KUPCHYNSKY

Missing since August 1, 1991
If you have any information
Contact GREECE POLICE, Monroe County, N.Y.

(716) 225-2525

11

The story of Stephanie's life is a game of connect-the-dots. It just takes me time to connect them, and the hues and shades of who she was start to fill into a complete portrait, even though it's still only in two dimensions. It is her murder that will ultimately define her—that will set her apart, that will draw attention to her life. But the story of her murder is a rabbit warren, a maze with a hundred dead ends. In my quest to understand my stepsister, I become a detective too, looking for meaning, for truth. For anything.

When I first started writing about Stephanie back in 2009, aimlessly trying to make sense of her dominion of my mind, my mom gave me a big canvas tote bag full of folders of articles and letters Jerry had organized by year, the last labeled "Stephanie—Final." I scrutinized every story, every page. So of course there was a lot I knew before I ever met DA Sandra Doorley.

After my trips to Rochester and D.C. in the summer of 2015, I need to be away from the distractions of New York City—the beach, my friends, dating, all of it. So I spend three weeks in that cabin in southern Vermont, surrounded by green. There's a porch where I sit during the day that overlooks a stream, and that view, that stream, coalesces with my imaginings of the terrain where Stephanie was found. My only writing buddies are a deer and a fox who come by each evening before I make dinner. My routine is simple, monastic almost. I eat, drink a glass or two of wine as I reread anything I've managed to write, and climb the steep stairs to the loft bedroom.

I spend most of my time either on the phone with Stephanie's friends, or scouring the over seven hundred files on the CD Sandra handed me that day in her office. The files are numbered in no sensible order, with no descriptions, so as I read every single one, I rename it. In the end I have a massive index of points of reference for the investigation into Stephanie's disappearance. "Dave Connors first three days." "Map of Northampton Park with Shawcross locations." "Jiffy Lube receipt July 31."

I want to absorb anything and everything connected to Stephanie's disappearance. I think if I can grasp the facts of her death, maybe her life will begin to become real too. Maybe if I can inculcate myself in the minutiae, somehow the insight I seek will be attainable. There is a way in somewhere among these forms and notes and records, I think.

And that's how I find myself, via their own written words in the sea of records on Sandra's CD, in the minds of two men whose lives were indelibly marked by Stephanie's life and death: Tom, the boyfriend who found his girlfriend's apartment empty, and Sergeant David Connors, the man who became as fixated on finding Stephanie originally as I am now.

12

Here's the version of events Tom told the police:

That first night after she went missing, Friday, August 2, 1991, he paced, his breath quickening, outside Stephanie's apartment building. If it had been during the school year, and Stephanie hadn't shown up for work, someone might have noticed sooner. But Stephanie had only missed a few lessons. Maybe she'd forgotten or made other plans. It was summer vacation; the students weren't worried. But Tom was.

He decided to drive to his sister Dee's house. But Dee hadn't heard from Stephanie. Neither had his sister Molly.

"Molly," Tom said, "something's wrong."

Molly suggested he call Maxine, who told him she'd seen Stephanie two nights earlier. "I have keys to her apartment," Maxine told him. So he drove to Maxine's place.

"Do you think she's mad at me?" he asked, standing in the doorway. He couldn't imagine why she would be, but there was no other explanation for her sudden disappearance.

Just two days earlier, Maxine had seen the sun shine on Stephanie's face as she laughed, holding her ice cream cone, and said, "Maybe I'll move to Ithaca!"

Maxine shook her head. "Not at all, Tom," she told him.

★

TOM LET HIMSELF into Stephanie's place, nervous about what he would find. He saw a bottle of Poland Spring water, full and unopened, on the floor in the doorway to the kitchen. Her violin was next to her open music stand, poised to be played. The pillows were neatly arranged on the bed, sheets folded on a nearby chair as though the bed was about to be made. The coffee maker was set up to brew morning coffee at the push of a button. Chubie and the parakeets twittered in their cages. Everything waited for the touch of Stephanie's hands. But there was no Stephanie.

Tom pressed play on the answering machine. Kids and their parents, their voices glib, wondering where Stephanie was and why she'd missed their Thursday lessons. His gut felt tight as he sat on the couch and stared at the wall, trying to think of what to do next and drawing blanks.

Tom called Maxine and Molly again, hoping they'd heard from Stephanie or had more of an idea of how to move forward than he did. He also called Stephanie's student Heidi's mother, who was just as dumbfounded as he was.

At 8:54 P.M. he called Jerry Kupchynsky, whom he'd never met and to whom he'd never spoken. Stephanie was supposed to be driving to New Jersey the next morning to teach at Jerry's conference, and Jerry had last heard from her when she left a message Wednesday night. He'd assumed he would see her when she arrived at the conference.

Jerry suggested calling the police soon. He and Tom spoke seven times that night. Tom also dialed information for Melanie, Stephanie's sister, living in Chicago, and called her twice; she didn't answer.

Next he looked in Stephanie's address book and called a few of Stephanie's friends in Martha's Vineyard; no one there had heard from her. He called Park Ridge Hospital to ask if there had been an accident. There hadn't. He called Maxine again around 11:00. "I still can't find her," he said.

"Maybe it's a good idea to call the police now," she said.

An hour later, Tom sat across from a Greece police officer in Stephanie's halogen-lit apartment as the officer began a missing persons report. It was 12:01 A.M. on August 3. The apartment that was so familiar to Tom—the couch he had lain on with Stephanie in his arms, the kitchen where she made him coffee with Chubie perched on her shoulder—had become this scene of tense bureaucracy.

Tom said it was uncharacteristic of Stephanie to have broken appointments; he wondered if she was in the midst of some sort of mental health episode. "She actually stopped taking her Prozac a few days ago, so I'm worried. We haven't spoken since Wednesday," he said.

In fact, it had been Tuesday when they spoke—one of the glitches in his story that later raised the cops' hackles.

When the official forms were finished, Tom climbed into the squad car in a daze. They went to see if Stephanie's car was parked at the Tops market on Maiden Lane, two miles away, where Stephanie often shopped. It wasn't there. The officer returned Tom to Stephanie's place in Newcastle Apartments and said they'd call him with any updates.

Alone again, Tom leafed through Stephanie's address book again and found a number for her new therapist, Pamela Rodgers. He dialed the number at about 3:00 A.M., and a groggy woman answered the phone. He explained who he was, though of course she had heard his name before.

"Stephanie is missing," he said, hoping she might have some insight.

"We should retrace her steps," Pamela replied. "But you need to sleep. People will be counting on you." He tried to sleep in Stephanie's bed; instead, he kept awaking in intense panics.

On Saturday morning, not sure if he'd slept at all, he called the Greece police again. "An APB is going out at eight, but really, Mr. Redmond, nothing suggests foul play," said the voice on the other end.

To Tom, the cops seemed nonchalant. That same weekend in Greece, there had been a home invasion and sexual assault, as well as a burglary and shooting that left one person permanently paralyzed. A missing persons report like this was neither uncommon nor alarming, the police said. Stephanie probably needed a break and was somewhere with a friend or alone to collect her thoughts. That was usually how these things turned out, they said.

"She wouldn't do this to me," Tom insisted when he called them again. They listened with disinterest, and he hung up the phone each time feeling almost spurned.

There was a blizzard of phone calls to and from Stephanie's landline that left Tom feeling tired and disoriented, unsure to whom he'd spoken.

Stephanie's car at the airport, 1991

Somehow Molly, Dee, and Tom's brother Niall materialized in Stephanie's apartment.

As they talked through plans and possibilities, Stephanie's therapist called with an idea. "Look for the car yourselves. Check the airport, the bus terminals, the malls."

At about 1:00 A.M. on August 4, Niall and his wife began combing the airport parking lots. They found three red Sentras and scrawled down the license plate numbers. Back at home, Niall checked that slip of paper against the number Tom had read to him over the phone that morning. He dialed Stephanie's phone number.

"I found her car," he told Tom.

★

IN A DAZE, Tom found himself back in a squad car, this time being driven to the airport. He recognized the Nissan immediately. "Yes," he said, not quite able to believe his eyes. "That's Steph's car."

The officers slim-jimmed the door open. Inside they found a shopping bag in the back seat, and two disconcerting details. The first was Stephanie's wallet, with her credit cards and ID, in the glove compartment. If she'd flown somewhere, even just to escape for a while, wouldn't she need her wallet? The second thing was the driver's seat, which had been pushed all the way back. Too far for Stephanie, who was only five foot four, to reach the pedals. Was someone else driving?

Tom watched as the Sentra was towed away. An officer's voice broke through his haze, saying not to worry. Stephanie was young, she'd probably met someone in a bar. "It happens all the time," the officer said. She'd show up soon.

Overwhelmed and unable to think clearly, Tom went back to Stephanie's apartment to call Jerry. Then, maybe, he slept. He wasn't sure.

"She's allowed, as an adult, to do whatever she wants," the police kept saying. But Tom, Dee, and Molly insisted this was not their Stephanie. Something terrible has happened, they repeated.

"Please stop calling so much," someone at the station told Tom.

In desperation, Tom and his sisters decided to muster the media's power. Around 10:00 A.M. that Sunday, August 4, Tom called Channel 13, Rochester's ABC network, and spoke to an assignment editor.

"My girlfriend is missing," he said. He asked if they'd air the story on the evening news. Anything might help.

That evening Tom retold his story on camera, the same one he had told the police and would tell again and again, adding that Stephanie's car had been found at the airport with the keys gone and her wallet in the glove box.

At some point soon after Melanie and her husband, Ed, arrived—Tom couldn't remember when, maybe a day or two after his interview for Channel 13—Tom went into Stephanie's room for a nap. Picking up one of the pillows, he noticed a small stain on the bare mattress.

"I called Mel in to look at it. I can't remember who else was there," he wrote in his statement. "We started looking around the room. I finally picked up the sheets from the chair. They were twin-size. They weren't for her bed; they were for her trip to New Jersey."

In a nauseating epiphany, they realized that the sheets from her bed were missing—that they had been missing the whole time.

13

TWENTY-FOUR YEARS AFTER Stephanie's disappearance, Sergeant David Connors and I drink coffee on a Rochester sidewalk in a light drizzle. It is the day after my meeting with Sandra Doorley. Sergeant Connors, a tall, slim, sharp-eyed, stolid man with close-cropped dark hair and an understated, deliberate cadence to his voice, seems reserved, almost suspicious of me, albeit in an amiable way. I can see I won't get much information from him without proving myself worthy, and I need to, since he's the original lead detective on Stephanie's case. He's also the only one of the case's original four detectives—David Connors, Dennis Armstrong, Michael Murray, and Don Farrell—I've been able to track down.

I ask Connors what he remembers of those first few days after the missing persons report was filed early Saturday morning, August 3. He says, "By Monday, it was going full steam ahead."

When Tom called the police about Stephanie's missing bedsheets, Sergeants Farrell and Murray reported to Stephanie's apartment. They took with them the stained mattress pad and the clothes Stephanie had worn when she visited Maxine—the white shirt and flowered shorts. They recorded the comforter and sheets as missing. They rifled through Stephanie's papers, looking for any scrap of information. They found a small amount of marijuana.

Technicians ran tests on the mattress pad and clothing, but learned nothing. The stain was human blood, but it couldn't be typed and was faded, suggesting it had been washed.

Now the cops were taking the case more seriously. The police cataloged the contents of Stephanie's car, a cluttered montage of her life. Sunglasses. Coffee-flavored lozenges. Receipts from Lee's dry cleaners. Envelopes and receipts from addresses in Martha's Vineyard and Ukraine. Insurance and AAA cards. Welcome Wagon certificates from Classic Hair, Buckman's Bakery, and Sugar Creek Convenience Store. A map of Massachusetts. A subscription card for *Glamour* magazine. A red umbrella. A dinosaur-shaped ice scraper. A Paula Abdul cassette case. Two heart-shaped crystal dishes. A plastic bag filled with teddy bear and treble clef figurines. A roll of wrapping paper. A Christmas ornament—Garfield the Cat, her dad's favorite.

The cops interviewed Tom for hours at a time. They called his land-lady, with whom he'd sit on the porch on summer evenings. She'd never heard him get up during the night, she said. But on the Friday that Tom rushed to Greece to find Stephanie missing, he'd told her, "I've got to go. My girlfriend is waiting."

They called Tom's coworker, who said his demeanor had not seemed strange the week Stephanie went missing, and that some work he'd done on a viola was "better than he would expect." They combed through his phone records. Tom said he'd last spoken to Stephanie on Wednesday, August 31, but there was no record of that call, either from him to her or the other way around. Their suspicion flared; what else wasn't true?

The police also knew Tom had gone to Northampton Park, asking questions. Tom himself told Farrell he'd "wandered into" the park back on August 6 and spoken to a park employee. That employee said Tom had shown up saying he was looking for any trace of Stephanie. "She might have lost it and left for a while," Tom had told him. The man had given Tom a map of the park, but Tom didn't take it. "I know the trails," he'd said. He'd returned after three hours, thanked the man, and left. The cops wondered what else Tom knew.

★

TOM WASN'T THE only one in the cops' crosshairs. On August 8, just over a week after Stephanie was last seen, the Brockport PD contacted Sergeant Dennis Armstrong. A teenager named Chris Mosher had walked right up to a Brockport police cruiser and handed over Stephanie's checkbook.

Chris Mosher had always been a fantasy-prone kid, his stepmother told Sergeant Connors. At nineteen, he often referred to fictional characters or women in his *Playboy* magazines as his girlfriends and used their names in passing as though the relationships were real. Lately he'd been making claims about having a girlfriend, although his stepmother didn't think he'd ever had one, didn't even think he'd had much physical contact with any woman. He had always been a little slow and didn't "function within reality," she said.

Chris felt he was old enough to be on his own, so he'd taken to sleeping in his car or on the beach at Hamlin Beach State Park in a tent. He hadn't been home for a good six weeks. Sometime in July, though, Chris had lost his job at Wegman's in Brockport, a small town thirteen miles west of Greece, close to Holley. He was hurting for money.

On Friday, August 2, Chris brought his black '82 Ford Escort to the Midas Muffler Repair shop in Brockport. The manager reported that he'd told Chris the cost of the brake repairs needed was $163.70. Chris wrote a check from his own checkbook, but the manager was suspicious and checked with the bank, finding that Chris's account was insufficient. "You'll have to come back with cash," the manager said. Chris left the car there.

On Sunday, August 4, Chris rode his bike over to his friend Todd's house in the afternoon, showing off a checkbook he was carrying around in his back pocket. Todd said Chris boasted, "Good thing I have a fiancée. She lets me write out her checks." He told Todd he lived with her in an apartment complex called the Meadows.

On Monday, August 5, Chris returned to Midas with a check for $165.79. Noticing a woman's name on the check and what looked like "a lot of scribbling," the manager refused it, too. Chris took off on his bike. He returned to the Midas shop with exactly $165.80 in cash, and left with his car.

Chris was back at Todd's house later that week, this time in his car. Todd saw a gold ring with a heart made of small diamonds in a jewelry box in the glove compartment. It was nothing too fancy, but Todd wondered how Chris could afford it. "It's for my fiancée," Chris told him.

After the Brockport PD contacted them on August 8, Farrell and Murray planned to meet Chris the next morning. It was clear to every police officer who spoke to Chris that they were dealing with someone with legitimate "cognitive difficulties," someone who might not quite understand the implications of his actions. Some wondered if they had a suspect in their missing persons case.

The morning of August 9, Farrell and Murray read Chris his Miranda rights, which he waived. He signed a search and seizure waiver allowing them to search his car; they found nothing.

This is the story Chris told: desperate for money, he'd spent the morning of Thursday, August 1, riding his bike around aimlessly, somewhere near Northampton Park, when he noticed a checkbook in the grass on the roadside. Without thinking, he scooped it up. Later that day, he went to the Columbia Bank in Brockport and wrote himself a check for $170.00 from Stephanie's checkbook. The teller knew Chris by sight, so she gave him the cash. He did the same the next Monday when he needed cash for his car, scrawling "Stephanie J. Kupchynsky" as payer.

"I knew it was wrong, and I was so sorry," Chris said. Regret nagged at him. That's why he had turned in the checkbook, he said.

With the obedience of a small child, he brought the police to the place he claimed he'd found the checkbook. He plunged his hands into the shrubbery and pulled out a deposit slip and check register that lay in the dirt, zeroing in with remarkable accuracy. A K-9 unit reported to the location with a German shepherd named Axel; the dog searched the surrounding fields and found nothing.

At a nearby McDonald's, Sergeants Connors and Armstrong bought Chris some French fries. As he ate, they asked if he had any information about where Stephanie was. Between bites, he told them he'd met and spoken to her, then later said he'd never met her and knew nothing about her. "Maybe you should search in Northampton Park," Chris said, and it sounded to the cops as if he knew they'd find something.

Chris was arrested and charged with forgery and petit larceny—all they really had on him. While he awaited trial at the county jail, Chris earned the nickname "Killer" from the other prisoners. They knew the checks he'd forged had belonged to the missing music teacher. But a fellow prisoner said Chris confided during a card game that he had nothing to do with her disappearance.

When Connors visited the Meadows, where Chris told Todd he lived with his "fiancée," the apartment manager didn't recognize Chris's face or name.

Nothing about this made sense. Chris was a blank. He insisted he knew nothing, and Connors didn't have enough to tie him to Stephanie's disappearance, but it was such a coincidence; the kid needed money and miraculously found it. He'd told his friend the checkbook was his fiancée's—but could it all have been a fantasy?

In the end, there was nothing: no evidence Mosher had ever encountered Stephanie before, no witness who'd seen him anywhere near her or her apartment. No legitimate motive, no connection at all. The timing of the check was deeply troubling—but to Connors, the boy didn't seem capable of murder.

Regardless, the moment that checkbook appeared, the stakes were raised. It didn't seem likely anymore that Stephanie was just shacked up with some guy. How had her checkbook wound up on the side of the road like that? Had she thrown it out the car window while someone with longer legs drove her car—as a signal for help, a beacon declaring that she was still alive?

14

O N SUNDAY, AUGUST 4, Stephanie's brother-in-law, Ed—Melanie's husband—went to the airport with a photo of Stephanie.

An employee at the Budget car rental counter told the police that on the night of August 1 at about 8:00, a woman asked about car rental prices. When the employee said there were no cars available, the woman asked about the shuttle bus to long-term parking and went outside. "I'm sure it was her," she said, looking at Stephanie's photo.

A shuttle bus driver said that on the same night, he'd picked up a passenger from the long-term parking lot who looked like the woman in the photo. "I know it was Thursday," the driver said, "I was hungover because on Wednesday—that's my day off—I got shit-faced."

The woman wore blue and carried two pieces of luggage. One, he said, was made of blue-and-white cloth, the other smaller and brown. Ed and Tom had reported a cloth suitcase missing from Stephanie's apartment.

The driver remembered saying hello, and that the woman responded with a small "Hi." She seemed "depressed and nervous," the driver said, and was wringing her hands and staring at the floor. She got out at the departure level.

The stories lined up. A flight had left the Greater Rochester International Airport that night, bound for LaGuardia, at 11:30, and another slightly earlier to Buffalo. Sergeant Farrell checked the flights' registers; Stephanie's name was absent. Still, Sergeant Armstrong wrote in his report, "On its face, the information is significant."

Another woman, who worked for a local security company, claimed she'd seen Stephanie near the security gate at the airport on Friday, talking closely with a man for about fifteen minutes.

Maybe Stephanie had up and flown away.

★

"WHY DON'T WE hear from SK's father?" Connors wrote in his notebook.

Back in East Brunswick, Jerry was surviving day by day, pushing forward as if things were normal. It was the same way that, as a child, he had survived Stalin's systematic starvation of the Ukrainian people, the way his mother had survived losing him for a month in Bavaria in a displaced persons camp, the way he'd survived being taken by force to a factory in Austria to scrub floors. It was the way he'd survived his service in the Korean War, during which his first wife, Gwylla, sent him a Dear John letter, having rethought the marriage in his absence. Now his daughter was missing, yet Jerry was still running the ASTA summer string camp that Stephanie and Tom were set to attend, teaching his summer lessons, and preparing for the beginning of the new school year.

When Sergeant Connors called, Jerry told him how happy Stephanie seemed with Tom, how he had advised her not to rush into anything. "He is a decent man, probably the man my daughter would marry," Jerry said, and added that Tom's treatment of Stephanie's beloved birds had been a good sign, a kind of trial marriage. "I'm clinging to hope she just had a bad reaction to going off the Prozac," he said.

The longer Stephanie was missing, the more her family began to fear the worst. In mid-August Jerry hired a private eye, frustrated at the lack of progress on the part of the police.

A few weeks later, an article appeared in the *East Brunswick Sentinel* with the headline "Man Asks for Public's Help to Locate Missing Daughter." Jerry spoke of Stephanie's depression and medication, but didn't seem to know all the possible reasons she'd left Martha's Vineyard: "It was a beautiful place during the summer, but in the winter, most people her age wouldn't stay. She decided she wouldn't spend another summer there and took the job in Greece."

Jerry wasn't the only one to wonder about Stephanie's mental state. Stephanie had made a dentist appointment for July 30. But on the twenty-ninth, the receptionist remembered, Stephanie showed up at the office. She seemed "confused, upset, and scatter-brained. . . . Her eyes looked funny. She acted strange, as if she wanted direction." The receptionist corrected Stephanie's scheduling error. When Stephanie returned the next day, July 30, she "was hyper" and "did not seem okay."

The band teacher said Stephanie seemed "air-headed" and had told him about her "bed-ridden mother and strict father." He shared an odd memory of a time Stephanie had said, "Today is a good day to take some drugs." Another coworker said Stephanie seemed "in a different world."

Connors tried to get a handle on the missing woman's mindset and what could have possibly led to her disappearance. He brainstormed in his notebook. "Why is car at airport? 1) She left it there to catch a plane. 2) She left it there to create hoax. 3) Someone else left it there to confuse investigation. Someone close to SK. KS or another lover. This person must have knowledge of pending trip. Otherwise car would be dumped elsewhere."

The police analyzed phone records, receipts from Stephanie's car, security cameras. Nothing turned up. Time passed, and all the leads the police had were paper tigers.

★

WITH EVERY LEAD that came to no fruition, Connors was disappointed, yet he kept trying to engage the case. Any lead might be the one he needed. When he noted that no one had a copy of the long-term parking log, he wrote in his notebook "Get a goddamned copy!"

He drove the route Stephanie took her last day, stopping to interview the owners of Lee's dry cleaners, measuring mileage that, according to Jiffy Lube's records of Stephanie's odometer, didn't add up. He canvassed her neighborhood. He ran priors on everyone living in the apartment building. He drew sketches of the locations in Northampton Park, where he knew Tom had gone looking around, claiming to "know the trails." It was the same park where serial killer Arthur Shawcross had dumped the bodies of his victims less than two years before.

Shawcross had been in jail for over a year already, but maybe he had an accomplice who was still out there. Or maybe a copycat was at work.

15

ROCHESTER AND ITS surrounding areas have seen their share of killers.

"Rochester is a violent place," Stan said to me once.

"What's wrong with Rochester?" I asked.

"Maybe a bad omen, a curse? It is remarkable the people who have come through there. Do you know how many serial killers came through Rochester? The Double Initial guy, the French race-car driver, the little twerpy guy out on Long Island, John White, who was never charged for killing prostitutes, Shawcross . . ."

But the murder that stands out the most for Stan is Stephanie's.

I look them all up later.

The Double Initial Killer, also known as the Alphabet Killer, raped and strangled three Rochester area girls between 1971 and 1973. Each of the girls—one aged ten and two aged eleven—had matching initials and was found in a town beginning with the same letter, miles away from where she'd been abducted. Carmen Colon was the first to go missing, in November 1971; her body was found two days later in Churchville. Wanda Walkowicz disappeared in April 1973, and was found the next day in Webster. Seven months later, Michelle Maenza was found in Macedon.

The killer has never been caught, though authorities suspected Kenneth Bianchi, who was later identified with his cousin as California's Hillside Stranglers. Bianchi was born in Rochester and moved to L.A. in 1977. A troubled child who suffered from seizures and bed-wetting, he killed ten women with his cousin Angelo Buono before Bianchi moved to Washington by himself and, without his cousin's help, murdered two more women. His carelessness as a solo offender is what led to his and his cousin's arrests. Attempts were made to connect Bianchi to the Double Initial murders in New York, but authorities lacked the forensic evidence to make the case stick.

Joseph Naso, another Rochester native, was the most recent person of interest in the Double Initial case. He was found guilty in 2013 of killing four sex workers in the late 1970s and early 1990s in California, and sentenced to death. Those women, too, all had the same first and last initials. Eerily, one was also named Carmen Colon. The others were Roxene Roggasch, Pamela Parsons, and Tracy Tafoya. But the DNA on Naso's victim's bodies didn't match the DNA found on the girls killed in Rochester.

The "French race-car driver" Stan brought up is actually an Australian—Christopher Wilder, the Beauty Queen Killer, a wealthy photographer and race-car aficionado who went on a wild killing and raping spree in 1984, raping at least ten women and killing at least eight. His MO involved attracting women by promising to photograph them and make them famous. He drove one of his victims, sixteen-year-old Tina Marie Risico, across the country with him, using her to lure another girl, Dawnette Wilt of Gary, Indiana, and brought both women to upstate New York. After stabbing Wilt and leaving her for dead (she miraculously survived), Wilder then used Risico again outside Rochester, luring another woman, Beth Dodge, whom he raped and shot, then dumped in a gravel pit before driving Risico to Boston's Logan Airport and releasing her. He was near the Canadian border in New Hampshire when state troopers caught and killed him with a single shot.

Joel Rifkin is "the little twerpy guy out on Long Island" Stan Chizuk mentioned. Adopted at two weeks old, Rifkin was an unathletic, dyslexic, bullied teen who went on to terrorize Long Island. But before his dark descent, he went to SUNY Brockport for a time, about halfway between where Stephanie lived and where her body was found. After killing seventeen women, perhaps more—all sex workers from the Long Island and New York City area—Rifkin was caught when police pulled him over for a missing license plate and caught wind of the stench of a rotting corpse in the trunk of his car. In his bedroom at his mother's house, police found newspaper clippings about Rochester's Arthur Shawcross and a book about the Green River Killer (identified as Gary Ridgway in 2001)—both men with a penchant for slaying sex workers. Rifkin is serving a sentence of 203 years at the Clinton Correctional Facility in New York. He is not eligible for parole.

John White was the man suspected in the deaths of several sex workers whose bodies were found near the Ontario State Parkway in 1992. The bodies began surfacing in May of that year, and resulted in a summer crackdown on the rampant prostitution near the intersection of Lake and Lyell Avenues in Rochester.

White was known for picking up sex workers and, instead of having sex, asking them questions about themselves and preaching to them before killing them. (He kept a Bible on his dashboard.) Two women escaped after he attacked them. Another—the sister of one of his alleged victims—recounted being picked up and questioned by White on three occasions. Police grilled him for fourteen hours, later "befriending" him, even buying him drinks at a bar, but they couldn't garner enough information for an arrest. Victim Glenda Crittenden's shoe and ring and victim Sandra Johnson's blood were found in White's truck; all of the women's remains were found in areas where White had either lived or fished; the Bible found in his car had passages about prostitution underlined. Killings with the same MO died down after White knew he was a suspect. Despite all this, he was never charged. In the fall of 1994, while police worked to collect more evidence, John White died of a heart attack.

The area has spawned even more killers than Stan mentioned. There's Robert Spahalski, who confessed in 2005 to killing four people in Rochester and Webster—at least two of them sex workers. And there's the man who true crime author Michael Benson calls "the Killer at Genesee Junction," who mutilated and killed his two teenage friends in his hometown of Chili (pronounced Chie-lie), right outside Rochester, in 1966, and who remains unidentified fifty-five years later.

★

BUT ARTHUR SHAWCROSS, who had dumped victims' bodies in the Northampton Park, is Monroe County's most infamous killer. In 1972, at age twenty-seven, Shawcross confessed to killing two children— Jack Owen Blake and Karen Ann Hill—in Watertown, New York. He was found guilty of manslaughter for one of the two, after striking a deal in exchange for disclosing the location of one of the victims' bodies.

After serving only fifteen years of his twenty-five year sentence, Shawcross was paroled, and set up in the Rochester area. He was forty-two. He was exactly six feet tall, with a doughy face, a bulbous nose, a double chin, and small, mud-colored eyes that blinked and squinted nervously as he spoke.

Shawcross claimed to have been sexually abused as a child by his mother and aunt. He also said he'd had a sexual relationship with his sister, his cousin, and local boys and girls, and that he had raped, murdered, and cannibalized Vietnamese girls while in the army.

Between 1988 and 1990 he killed eleven women, mutilating several of the corpses, in the Rochester area. All but one were sex workers he picked up on Lyell Avenue in Rochester; their bodies were found in the woods and ravines near the Genesee River. In January 1990—mere months before Stephanie would move to an apartment less than twenty miles away—a police helicopter spotted the body of June Cicero in a viaduct in Northampton Park. Shawcross was seen standing on the road nearby, either urinating or masturbating. It was later determined that he had returned to the spot where he dumped June's body. The police released him after questioning, as they didn't have enough to arrest him, but the next day a hunter found the body of another victim, Felicia Stephens, in the park nearby. When the police canvassed several sex workers on Lyell Avenue, armed with a photo of Shawcross, several said they recognized him as a regular customer.

The police brought Shawcross in again. Threatening to involve his wife and mistress, they gave him another chance to confess. He protested that his girlfriend was not involved, and in doing so implicated himself. The police kept up the pressure, and he began to wear down; eventually he confessed to a total of eleven murders, explaining what each woman had "done" to deserve it—such as mocking him, talking too much, or simply reminding him of his mother.

Shawcross tried an insanity defense in his televised trial that November—just three months after Stephanie moved to Greece—intermittently talking in a high squeaky voice, saying his time in Vietnam had traumatized and destroyed him. But in the end, Shawcross was found guilty of all ten murders in Monroe County, and sentenced to twenty-five years for each, totaling 250 years. He died of cardiac arrest in 2008 after being moved to a hospital from the Sullivan Correctional Facility in Fallsburg, New York.

Northampton Park. Tom had gone there, and Chris Mosher had mentioned it, too. The Greece cops knew that was where Arthur Shawcross had disposed of his victims' bodies. Was Stephanie's body there too?

16

S UMMER TURNED TO fall, and the school year started without Stephanie. Connors and his colleagues still couldn't shake their hunch that Tom was involved in her disappearance. They asked him to take a polygraph, and he agreed.

On October 12, just over ten weeks since Stephanie had gone missing, polygraph operator Mark Sennett administered the test in a small room lit with fluorescent lights at the Greece PD. Sergeants Farrell and Murray watched through a two-way mirror.

During their pretest interview, Tom said Stephanie was the "love of his life" and talked about their future plans. Sennett made a note of how much Tom stressed the fact that he and Stephanie had many plans. This time, when Tom relayed the story of his proposal, he claimed that Stephanie had "said yes without hesitation," a change from the "Oh, Tom" he'd previously reported.

Sennett asked about the discrepancy regarding the date of the phone call the police were concerned with. Tom claimed he was confused. "I loved Stephanie," he said.

His use of the past tense didn't surprise Sennett, but Tom went on to justify it, anyway. "In my heart, I believe she is dead."

Sennett explained to Tom that the polygraph would ascertain if there were some aspect of the relationship about which Tom hadn't been forthright. Perhaps there'd been an argument or other conflict Tom had been afraid to share because it might make him seem culpable. Tom said he'd told nothing but the truth.

Sennett began placing the attachments onto Tom, and panic flashed across Tom's face. "Is there a problem?" Sennett asked, and Tom said no. "If you are being truthful, there won't be any problem," Sennett said.

Suddenly, several questions into the test, Tom halted. "I think I am 'responding' to the questions," he said. He was nervous that his disturbance might affect his test results. In his report later, Sennett, an experienced polygraph examiner, wrote, "This came unsolicited and seemed inappropriate." Tom looked more and more anxious to Sennett as they continued.

Sennett concluded that Tom's "responses appeared to indicate deception." His report reads, "In my opinion, he was not being completely truthful when denying further knowledge of Stephanie's disappearance or the circumstances surrounding it."

When Sennett told Tom the results, Tom just stared, saying nothing. "Did you kill Stephanie?" Sennett asked.

"No," Tom answered, his tone emotionless.

To Sergeant Farrell, who watched through a two-way mirror, Tom sounded "rehearsed" and was "measured and deliberate."

Farrell and Murray came in to question Tom about the day he'd gone poking around Northampton Park, telling the park ranger he knew the trails well. Sitting across from Tom, who was still seated after Sennett removed the polygraph attachments, Farrell asked, "How did you select Northampton Park?"

Tom said that while he was looking at an area map, he'd noticed the big green spot of the park and thought it would be a good place to check. "I was only there for an hour," he said.

Farrell knew he'd actually been there three hours. The ranger had kept tabs and told the cops so.

"Where in the park did you go?" Farrell asked.

Tom said nothing. Out of patience, Farrell jumped up from his chair in a rage and slammed down the map.

"Where is she?" he shouted, his voice echoing against the walls.

That question, and that moment, would haunt Tom forever.

★

SERGEANT FARRELL HAD already, at the end of August, conducted an air search of Northampton Park from a helicopter and spotted nothing. On October 20 Farrell led another search party in Northampton Park, this time with cadaver dogs. They trawled the woods and ravines of the nearly thousand-acre park, bigger even than New York City's Central Park, crunching through vibrant autumn leaves that might have been disguising anything underneath.

They did not find Stephanie.

Instead, they found a brown Esprit purse. It matched the description of Stephanie's missing one, the one Maxine and her daughter had seen her carrying that last day.

They'd found her checkbook, and now, less than a mile away, they'd found her purse.

The fact that Shawcross's victims had also been found nearby led them to imagine that they might be close to finding Stephanie. But it was not to be. If there was anything left to find, it was hidden well.

17

O N AUGUST 29, 1991, one month after Stephanie disappeared, Stephanie's high school friend Sharon called the Greece police. She told them that she was shocked by how much of a "goody-goody" Jerry had been made out to be by the media. In her opinion, he was a real "bastard" who beat Stephanie all the time. Back in school, Sharon's phone would ring late at night, and Stephanie would sob on the other end, scared her father was going to hit her again.

On September 5, another high school friend, Janine, called the Greece police for the same reason. She stated that Stephanie "was physically and mentally abused by her father," often came to school with bruises, and had been seeing a therapist since elementary school to deal with her trauma. She said Stephanie's friends were all intimidated and frightened by Jerry.

In disbelief, I read and reread their words in the troves of the CD Sandra gave me. I have to know more. I have to find out if my stepfather was not what I—and everyone I'd known, as far as I could tell—thought. The man I knew was quiet, if occasionally sullen, and bent in half by Parkinson's disease. One of the last times I saw him, to help my mother move him from his nursing home to hospice care in 2009, I sat close to his wheelchair and held his hand while he muttered in slurred Ukrainian.

"Jerry, you have to speak English to me. I don't speak Ukrainian, remember?" I said.

He picked up his head with effort, looking past me to survey the sunny, carpeted room filled with gray-haired ladies doing crossword puzzles in oversize floral-upholstered armchairs. In his thick accent, he whispered, "I'm trying to decide if those soldiers over there are German or American. Their uniforms don't look American."

There was nothing I could say. I suppose he had slipped back in time to when he was conscripted by the Nazi army during World War II, to some terrible place to which I had no access. This is the man I knew—vulnerable and diseased.

If I have any memories that might hint that my stepfather could be so volatile, I must have quashed them.

I find the women on Facebook. I email Stephanie's friend Janine, send her a screen shot of the police report. She can't remember a thing. She sees her name and old phone number, recognizes her phrasing, but can't remember actually placing the call. She remembers Stephanie, her sweetness and brightness, but can't believe she was able to forget "that kind of fuckery." Over the weeks we email, a vision comes to her mind of Stephanie's thin, pale skin etched over with bruises she assumed came from Jerry, but the years have eroded anything else.

When I get in touch with Sharon, she remembers everything in a flood. She is still overcome with grief. I think she's retreated when I don't hear back from her for a few days, but she is on her own mission. She tracks down five or six other friends of Stephanie's who corroborate her account of Jerry's cruelty. She's never forgotten Stephanie's desperate phone calls.

Stephanie shared her suffering with her friends only piecemeal. One by one, they tell me about my stepfather's abuse of Stephanie. I want to deny it; I've always thought of Jerry as an improvement—at least in temperament—on my own tyrannical, sadistic father. But the weight of all their recollections cumulate in an undeniable realization that she was, like me, the daughter of an abusive father.

"Stephanie told me, 'I have the perfect sister, and I'm the bad one,'" says Lisa, one of the friends Sharon has collected for me. "She showed me Melanie's report cards—nothing but straight A's."

Stephanie confided that her parents once told her that her birth triggered her mother's multiple sclerosis. Whether they told her this to be cruel or because they didn't understand the effect it might have, I don't know. The emotional toll drove Stephanie into therapy.

She once showed Lisa her back, covered in welts and bruises, after she was beaten with a belt. Lisa says she wasn't shocked. She'd been at the Kupchynsky house when Jerry yelled at Stephanie as if Lisa weren't even there.

Jerry put the kibosh on Stephanie's friendships and flirtations, her friend Holly tells me. Stephanie was so hypervigilant, always jumpy and looking over her shoulder. And around Stephanie's eye one day at school was a noticeable black-and-blue circle. Everybody knew her dad did it. Holly asked, anyway.

"I got it at home," Stephanie said quietly. "Holly, I want to tell you something. You swear you'll never tell anyone?"

Stephanie confided that, in Holly's words, "her father beat the snot out of her" on a regular basis. "While Stephanie's father was getting all the accolades," Holly says, "she was getting her ass kicked."

Then Holly tells me that when she first heard about Stephanie's disappearance, she thought, "She was finally going to tell about her dad, and he snapped and killed her."

I check with friends from other times, later times, to see if Stephanie ever talked about her childhood abuse as an adult. Nancy, the mom who brought Stephanie to teach on Martha's Vineyard, tells me Stephanie said that when she was a kid, Jerry would lock her in her room to practice. And Paula, Stephanie's confidante in Greece, tells me that Stephanie still seemed petrified of her father; she agonized over going to New Jersey, and it seemed to Paula that she only visited him out of obligation.

The sheer number of completely disconnected people who instantly divulge their memories of Stephanie's mistreatment and dread convince me it happened. But these increasingly legitimate facts still hurt to accept.

To think of the stepfather I knew—gruff, for sure, but tender, too—as capable of such ferocity is not easy. I call my mother from the porch of my Vermont cabin. She's getting used to my sporadic phone calls to ask for quick clarifications or small details I know she will remember. This time I'm asking her a more loaded question.

"Did you know anything about Jerry abusing Stephanie?"

She sighs matter-of-factly. "No, but it doesn't surprise me."

Her lack of surprise surprises me. I only ever saw her love him, dote on him, nurse him. I know of no strife between them, but she tells me that there were moments when he could be controlling, angry, possessive. I never knew.

★

JERRY'S LIFE HAD been a series of trials, where grit and backbone and a plain unwillingness to acquiesce were what allowed him to endure. He survived Nazis and Stalin, but the challenges of being a de facto single father must have been his Waterloo, especially when he had to confront in his daughter some of his own obstinacy. I believe Jerry loved Stephanie, but that he loved her imperfectly.

His tactics backfired. Her friends tell me the more he prodded Stephanie, the more she pushed back. The more austerity he administered, the more unruly she became. When he grounded her, she sneaked out. Like me, she responded to her father with ferocity. Like my father, he intensified his harshness. As a result, his draconian behavior created a rift between them, a rift that seemed obvious even to the friends she made in her late twenties.

As I learn about Stephanie, I recognize myself—and the traumas that worked their ways into the fibers of both our bodies.

The pain she was made to feel originated from her father. And she took it all in, learned the same delusional lessons I did—even if our fathers' objectives differed. We don't fully believe we can be adored, because the people who should have adored us, should have made us believe in our own lovability, instead told us we were worthless.

The pain she must have felt is one I know well. There's an inner voice that says I have no value, a voice that seems to be telling God's honest truth, a voice it's taken years to be able to even begin to think of as a liar. And there's my truer self, which fights to nurture and free itself.

Stephanie was drawn to men who let her keep hating herself. "I realized later," her friend Jane says, "when you have a 'bad father,' that's what you keep looking for."

Her friend Gail from Martha's Vineyard says that Stephanie turned her pain inward, becoming "a beacon for someone who's had similar experiences but who turned it into hurting others." She doesn't go into detail about what Stephanie's Martha's Vineyard boyfriend Geoff might have experienced as a little boy, so I am left to imagine them.

But this pattern of Stephanie's I recognize, too. More than one of my romantic relationships has erupted after sweet beginnings into abuse and violence. I've been pinned against walls, shoved onto floors, hit in the face, abandoned in the street, screamed at, called names, surveilled, and stalked—and each time it happens, I swear it will never happen again. And when it does, I am as shocked as I was the first time.

But I am years out now from the last one, and I swear it will never happen again.

★

I SPEAK WITH two other men who dated Stephanie—both seemingly sweet, gentle men. One is Phillip Brazer, a friend of Stephanie's friend Sharon. Phillip dated Stephanie in high school, Sharon says. It's hard to get him off the phone when I call him; all he wants to do is keep talking about her. He tells me the entire story of their brief high school relationship.

He knew what kind of guys Stephanie went for—tough guys, bad boys—and he didn't think he stood a chance with her. But he took a deep breath and asked her out one day after geometry class. She threw a real curveball back and said yes.

Phillip picked her up in his green 1970 Impala. He went in to meet Jerry and Jean; it seemed they were doing more than sizing him up. "I didn't like the feeling in that house," he tells me.

But Stephanie was happy all night. "This is my first real date," she told Phillip at dinner. To impress her, he'd bought tickets to a performance of *The Nutcracker Suite*.

When he pulled up outside her house afterward, Stephanie slid right across the bench seat and started kissing him. When she came up for air and went inside, he drove home ecstatic.

The next weekend, for their second date, Stephanie offered to come to Phillip's house when his parents were out. She pulled him by the hand into his bedroom. "This is it; we're going to do it," Phillip thought.

But without warning, she stopped. "I can't do this," she said. "You're too nice. I'm so sorry. There's this guy I've had a crush on for years, and he asked me out last week. We went out the other night, and I think I really might like him."

Phillip knew the guy. He knew how it would go.

"He's no good, Steph. I'm the one who cares about you!" he said, begging, but Stephanie got up from the bed, smoothed her hair, and walked out the door.

Late one Saturday night, Stephanie called Phillip from a party in tears, her speech slurred. "My father will kill me. I'm so drunk. I need you to come pick me up!"

Begrudgingly, Phillip drove to the party and brought her home. "You were right," she said. "He said the magic was gone."

She turned toward him, moved closer, nuzzling up to him. He stiffened and held her at bay.

"What's wrong? You were right; you're the one! I'm right here!" Her voice was getting louder.

"You hurt me, Steph," Phillip tried to explain. "It's too much for me."

Then, Philip says, Stephanie snapped. "You don't want me anymore?" she yelled, kicking the car door open in a huff. "What's your problem, anyway? What are you, gay or something?" She slammed the door and was gone for good.

"Maybe if I'd forgiven her, I would've married her, and none of this would've happened," Phillip tells me on the phone. It's a ridiculous theory. They went out twice. But Phillip is stuck on Stephanie. He wishes he could have saved her.

In Martha's Vineyard, before Geoff, Stephanie dated Keith Dodge, an English teacher who worked with her. When I email him, he says he'll be in New York for Thanksgiving, and do I want to meet him at Joe Allen's for brunch?

So I sit across the table from one of Stephanie's former lovers, ordering a Bloody Mary. "Are you sure you're not related?" he asks me. "You look just like her."

Soon he's telling me all he remembers of his short relationship with Stephanie, ten years his junior. They met on the ferry on a bright fall day, and he recognized her from school. They saw each other through the winter; later, he emails me a photo of the Valentine's Day card she gave him. "I'll tell you one thing—the sex was great," Keith says.

Their relationship was mostly light, mostly fun. But one night, he brought her home after a date, and he was tired. He told Stephanie he didn't want to stay at her place that night and would like to be alone. Stephanie shocked him with immediate fury, shrieking "You don't want to stay? Don't you realize every other boyfriend of mine *worshipped* me?"

Keith had to roll up the windows of his car as he drove off because Stephanie started throwing things at him. He was too independent to take on her tantrums. The incident was too much for him; it caused a complete and immediate split, he tells me. He never understood why she reacted so strongly, but by the time I meet Keith, I've learned that rage slumbered inside Stephanie, as it does in me, all the time.

★

SHARON AND JANINE weren't the only ones to think, back in 1991, that Jerry might have been a factor in Stephanie's disappearance.

"She planned this disappearance," Michele—the friend who'd rescued Stephanie from the bubble gum explosion in high school—says she thought. "She faked her own murder to get out from Mr. K."

Phillip's mind, too, went straight to Stephanie's father. "That was my initial response," he says.

Nancy, Stephanie's friend from Martha's Vineyard, was sure Stephanie would never take off from Greece on her own, even though, to her, it seemed like the explanation the police favored. Nancy couldn't believe Stephanie would leave her precious birds and violins without a word to her sister. But she did toy with the idea, when "the chances of her coming back seemed slim to none," that maybe Stephanie "committed suicide to get away from her father."

This line of thinking made some sense to the police, who found a copy of the self-help book *How to Break Your Addiction to a Person* in Stephanie's apartment, with some passages highlighted concerning escape.

I have never—not in all the time I learned about Stephanie, not in the midst of this new epiphany about her childhood—given much credence to the theories that Jerry had anything to do directly with her murder. Maybe that's because when other people do, it hurts me in ways I can't explain entirely. Half of me wants to defend my stepfather, and the other half wants to blame him for placing her on the path on which she wandered. My stepfather's abuse, in my mind, led Stephanie to Geoff. And Geoff pushed her to Greece, where she would meet her end.

Like me, she perhaps felt she had no real home, that she would always roam, that maybe she could not be loved. Like me, she learned to erupt quickly in moments that required more finesse.

It leaves me furious. Furious with my dead stepfather for beginning the lifetime of pain my ghost sister felt until she was killed, furious with my own dead father for beginning a lifetime of pain for me that makes it possible for me to connect so easily to Stephanie. Raging at the dead—an exercise so fruitless it leaves me furious with myself.

Stephanie and I had more in common than our eyes. I have sensed it all along. Is this what I sought to find, hidden in all this history?

When I committed to telling Stephanie's story, I didn't know what I would uncover. The moral implications of telling this part cause me to struggle, though I know I have to do it. I tell Stephanie's friend Paula this, when she tells me what she knows. "That's who she was," Paula says. "If you're not going to tell her whole story, why tell it at all?"

I repeat the line to myself.

Now over forty, I am still working at unraveling the knots of my childhood. Stephanie was killed when she was still a mass of insecurities and just beginning to take steps toward disentangling herself from the trauma.

"I don't really deserve to ever be happy," Stephanie once said to Paula as they walked along the shore of Lake Ontario.

Fastening her eyes on Stephanie's, Paula told her, "You deserve more than happiness. You deserve overwhelming joy."

★

SERGEANT DAVID CONNORS doubted that Jerry had anything to do with Stephanie's disappearance. He hadn't been anywhere near Rochester and was, if not distraught, at least very ruffled by his daughter's absence.

But he did keep the "unflattering references" in the back of his mind. He didn't buy into them, nor did he dismiss the information. At that early point, he tells me, "All options had to remain on the table."

Everyone had a theory.

Stephanie's friend Paula in Greece told the police everything she knew—about Geoff, the abortion, Stephanie's frequent suicidal musings. But Paula, like many others, said Stephanie was too enamored of her three pet birds to have abandoned them. The birds were like her children. And more than anything, Paula later tells me, "I was adamant that she would not have driven herself to the airport. I drove her to the airport when she flew anywhere. She was terrified of driving; all she wanted to do was drive to work and home again."

Then there were the people who felt sure something terrible had happened. Her high school friend Lisa remembers her mother suggesting that Stephanie had run off. "No," she tells me she told her mother, "Steph is way too dependent to run off on her own and live an individual life. No, something bad has happened to her. We've lost Stephanie."

Melanie once told me that from the moment her phone first rang in Chicago, she believed her sister was dead. And even Sergeant Farrell said in late August 1991, when interviewed by the *Home News* in New Jersey, "If she just took off, it seems she would have probably contacted someone by now."

But my stepfather never stopped asserting that she was alive, being held somewhere against her will, a sex slave or something like that. Even years later, in the few months after he'd married my mother and before Stephanie's bones were found, he would begin sentences, "When Stephanie comes back . . ."

My mother would say gently, "Jarema, if she does come back, she'll have been through something horrible. She'll need our help." And he'd shoo her away.

"My daughter is a professional. She'll be fine."

There was little reason to think she might have still been alive. But, almost maddeningly, there was no reason to believe she wasn't.

18

I F IT IS exhausting for me to compile and collate the sightings and leads and rumors, which continued for months, it must have been more maddening still for Connors and his team. Not only to make sense of it all, but to procure it all in the first place.

Stephanie was seen in a red car on the side of the road in Hamill, at a bar in Rochester, near the Steamship Authority in Martha's Vineyard, hitchhiking in Rochester, in a trailer park in nearby Parma, walking along the Ontario State Parkway talking to herself and gesticulating with her hands and arms, at a Burger King in Syracuse with a man who held a gun to her side and threatened to kill her, playing the violin for money in Toronto, playing the violin for money in Key West. One psychic said she was alive and well but had been sold to an Arab country, and another psychic said she was somewhere in the Eastman Theatre.

In November 1991 a woman called the nearby Gates PD to say her son's eleven-year-old friend claimed that he knew Stephanie was in South Carolina. The little boy said he'd overheard Stephanie talking to a man about her plans to go to South Carolina for a while. He hadn't said anything about it yet because he was afraid he'd get in trouble for eavesdropping. It was a strange lead because it came from a child—one who could have known Stephanie from school, who might be telling the truth. The boy's father, Edward Laraby, told the police his son had made it up and had "an active imagination."

On the advice of another psychic and a dowser, Jerry and Melanie, desperate enough to suspend their doubt, prevailed upon the Massasauga Search and Rescue Team to search Northampton Park again, areas in Adams Basin, and a pond in Hamlin with their cadaver dogs. They found nothing.

In February 1992 Sergeant Murray, who believed Stephanie was alive, made appearances on *A Current Affair* and *Hard Copy* to plead for information. Another psychic called to say Stephanie had taken a friend's kids out for ice cream in the Rochester area, and that she was "upside down in a barrel in a frozen river, creek, or pond." Yet another psychic said Stephanie could be found in the Erie Canal between Brooks and Chili Avenues. She said she was aware that several psychics were sure Stephanie would be found in or near water.

The Greece PD followed every lead. Connors knew that the more time passed, the less likely he was to find answers. But he kept circling back, going over everything. Every crackpot, every mystic, every outlandish phone call. Twenty-five years later, I shadow his moves. And I am just as bewildered by arguably the strangest sighting of all—in Poughkeepsie, New York, three hundred miles from Rochester.

★

"THERE WAS SOME kind of desire, or longing, in her eyes, a sexual, lonely feeling," said the anonymous voice on the phone. He had first called on August 19 to say he'd seen Stephanie in a Dunkin' Donuts in Poughkeepsie. The police had gone on the news, asking for the anonymous caller to call a private line they set up just for him. Instead, skirting easy identification, the man called 911 and asked for the reporting sergeant.

Stephanie was with a woman who seemed "dominant and in charge," said the man, but she must not have wanted his help. "I'm the biggest and baddest guy for a couple of miles around," he bragged. "She could have easily gotten my help."

He saw her a second time, too, though he couldn't be sure if it was in the parking lot of a place called Bertie's Disco, where he'd stopped to look at some Harleys, or sitting with some "wimp" at the bar catty-corner to

Bertie's. Again, he said, they'd made "heavy eye contact." He couldn't get her out of his head, he said. "She was gorgeous."

The anonymous man chatted and boasted long enough for the police to track him down. A background check revealed a spotty criminal past and psychiatric issues. But it didn't matter, because there was something completely unexpected about this sighting that made it impossible to discount.

The connection was to Stephanie's first cousin Ivan Pavlak, the one with whom she'd just gone to Ukraine days before she vanished. He worked at Bertie's Disco, three hundred miles away from Greece, the same place this mystery caller said he had seen Stephanie.

When Connors and Armstrong went to interview the caller, he wrote in his statement, "I'm sure the girl I saw in Poughkeepsie is Stephanie Kupchynsky, I immediately recognized her on television that first night home."

Armstrong contacted Ivan, who told him about the recent trip to Ukraine, and said Stephanie told him she was happy at her job, loved her students, and was thrilled with her new boyfriend. She was always some-what "ditzy," Ivan said. He'd spoken with her twice since they returned, but she'd never been to Bertie's. He said police could check the security camera footage.

But at that small café in Rochester twenty-plus years later, Connors says to me, "What are the chances of this person calling about this place two hundred and fifty miles away in a bar he had no idea had any connection? How do you ignore that?"

They couldn't. And so, in April 1992, Armstrong and Connors trav-eled to Poughkeepsie and stayed the night, enlisting the help of an officer whose brother happened to live with Ivan Pavlak.

The officer questioned Ivan for more than two hours, during which Ivan again maintained he hadn't seen Stephanie after their trip and that, as far as he knew, she'd never been to Poughkeepsie, at least not before her disappearance.

Connors and Armstrong headed to Bertie's Disco. It matched their anonymous caller's description. A bouncer named John told them he thought he'd seen Stephanie in August, that he had a memory of her using her passport as ID.

But that was impossible; the police had had her passport since she vanished. This lead, too, went nowhere.

★

NEITHER ANYTHING THE police had discovered to that point nor the influx of claims, sightings, and theories they'd received from all over the country had helped move them any closer to finding Stephanie.

It would be years before Stephanie was found, as at least three psychics had predicted, submerged in water. I map the locations the psychics named. From Adams Basin to Hamlin, as the crow flies, is just short of nine miles. From Adams Basin to Holley—where Stephanie was found—is just over nine miles. From Hamlin to Holley is eight. As I look at the map, measuring with my eyes, the three locations create an eerie, near-equilateral triangle.

19

As luck would have it, when Connors tried to call Stephanie's ex on Martha's Vineyard, Geoff Fletcher, he learned that Geoff was visiting his parents in Hammondsport. That was only an hour and a half drive from Greece, as opposed to eight hours away off the coast of Massachusetts. On August 8, 1991, only five days after the missing persons report was filed, Connors drove to Hammondsport to talk to Geoff.

What about this guy, who, according to Stephanie's friends, more or less drove Stephanie off Martha's Vineyard and forced her to abort her pregnancy? Connors considered—and reconsidered—whether what her friends had to say was true.

She'd told some of them she still talked to him on the phone sometimes. Her therapist said she might be on Martha's Vineyard and told Connors of Stephanie's "secret trips out of town" and history of mental health problems.

Geoff said Stephanie could be manipulative, threatening suicide, throwing herself against walls and floors. He proceeded to tell Connors about the night she'd grabbed his loaded shotgun.

There was nothing to make police believe that Geoff had been responsible for Stephanie's disappearance; if anything, what he told them jibed with their theory that she may have been, like the title of that book they'd found suggested, trying to break her addiction to someone by just starting fresh somewhere new. So they didn't track down any more information about Geoff. But as with the other strange or uncanny characters he'd encountered, like Chris Mosher and Ivan Pavlak, Connors didn't dismiss him as a possible suspect, either.

★

TWENTY-FIVE YEARS LATER, I try and fail with Geoff as well. He refuses to answer my questions after I say I can't physically go to Florida, tosses around legal terms that feel like a threat, and expresses that he has an affinity for firearms. He is, even at almost seventy, the scariest person with whom I communicate. But he is also the one I most want to know more about.

On Martha's Vineyard that gray January in 2016, Officer Michael Gately and his wife, Betsy, drive me around the Vineyard, half sightseeing, half theorizing. "Here's John Belushi's grave . . ." Gately says, "Here's the school where your sister taught. . . . Here's where Carly Simon played a surprise gig once. . . . Here's where that bastard Geoff used to live . . . and how can we really be sure he had nothing to do with it?"

In fact, right after Melanie got to Greece to look for her sister, she'd called Stephanie's Vineyard friend Nancy, little Meg's mom, theorizing that Stephanie might be at Geoff's house. "Can you go there and look for her?" she asked.

Nancy wasn't worried at all, though, she tells me. She knew Geoff, and even though he was eccentric and his relationship with Stephanie a disaster, she didn't think he had anything to do with this.

Gately and his wife tell me to call Lee Fierro. The actress most famous for slapping Chief Brody after the death of her fictional son Alex in *Jaws*, Fierro knew Geoff back in his Island Theatre Workshop days. In fact, she was one of the founding members of that workshop.

So from my hotel room I look up her number, listed in the Martha's Vineyard phone book, and dial. I am shocked—and maybe a little starstruck—when she picks up right away. But all she really tells me is that the ladies loved him and he'd always been "somewhat of a Lothario."

"You'll hear a lot of misinformation about Geoff," Stephanie's friend and fellow string teacher Gail tells me on the phone. "Gossip was king" on Martha's Vineyard, and "the more interesting story always trumped the truth." Rumors flew around about Geoff, and after his two subsequent fiery affairs, he left the island, too.

But some people, even ones who knew him well, stand firm in their belief—to this day—that Geoff was involved. One of those people—a person too scared to give a name—says to me, "I still think it was Geoff and nothing will change that."

Then, in December 2018, out of nowhere, Geoff emails me. Having lost his job with the Naples Orchestra and Chorus in Florida a few years earlier over "personality conflicts," according to an article in the *Naples Daily News*, he's decided to move back to New York and is living in Canandaigua, just north of Rochester. He feels different about sharing his stories with me, he says, after reading some of my essays and finding me "inquisitive and unbiased, interested in the fabric, texture, and meaning of relationship."

He tells me about the night Stephanie "threatened him with a shotgun and ran barefoot back to her house" and then began "screaming about killing herself" on the phone. He tells me about the abortion; in Geoff's version, "after much conversation, she agreed to an abortion," even though he "knew it was not what she wanted." But, Geoff writes, in his opinion, Stephanie was "too crazy" to be a mother.

There is also a great deal of guilt expressed in his email: "I deeply regret that my own issues played into reinforcing her bad childhood. I know I was blinded by my sexist attitudes at the time. I do carry the awful reality of the part I played in Stephanie's life and her choice to leave [Martha's Vineyard] thereby exposing herself to abduction and death."

He now says he finds other stories about Stephanie "borderline delusional," a statement I found myself nodding to as I read, and that what he wants more than anything, just like I do, is "a true and balanced portrait of Stephanie and her family along with the forces and events leading to her tragic end."

I hate what he did to Stephanie, using his older age and imposing physicality (I never forget his domestic violence citations, the restraining orders) to coerce her into an abortion, and I hate his veiled legal threats and his guns. Still, three years after I first ask for his cooperation, twenty-seven years after her disappearance, Geoff writes, "In my mind the refrain of 'if only . . .' echoes and demands accountability. That is vastly different from guilt and regret but it comes with its own punishments. Even though I can look at the past and see myself as moved by forces in myself I did not understand, I accept my accountability in this tragedy."

It seems like maybe Geoff has acknowledged the role his own traumas played in the way he treated Stephanie. I read his email with a cynicism nursed by my own history with men, by what I know about Geoff so far, wondering what he wants. At the same time, I want to believe there is authentic remorse in him for whatever he did. And if the remorse is real, perhaps so is his evolution.

20

W HEN THE SCHOOL year started in September 1991, I was a soph-
omore, and it would be five more years before my parents
divorced and we moved next door to Jerry. But I noticed him in the
corner of the band room or the back of the auditorium, checking in on
various ensembles. I took account of his stature, his face, as I tried to pay
attention to Mr. Whitlock's or Mr. Tedeschi's conducting. Everybody at
school knew what had happened, and my friends and I talked about his
courage and strength in pushing forward and holding onto hope.

Jerry Kupchynsky was a stoic man. It was a stoicism accumulated
from a lifetime of hardship: the abuse he'd endured at the hands of his
own stepfather, the strident disapproval of a mother who harped on him
until the day she died, the years he spent in a displaced persons camp in
Bavaria, his experiences when he'd been conscripted by the Nazis, his
nearly dying of pneumonia, his first wife's leaving him, his second wife's
multiple sclerosis . . . It was the only way he knew how to be.

But after Stephanie's disappearance, he changed. As the terrible lack
of knowledge about what had happened to her extended, his resolve
began to crack at the edges, although few could tell from the outside.

After two months, when it began to seem like Stephanie would not
soon resurface, and some people began to call it a "lost cause," waves of
correspondence began rolling in from all reaches of the country. These
letters are now all in a fat manila envelope in the bag of files my mother
gave me. I sit on the floor of my apartment when I get back to Brooklyn

from Vermont that summer of 2015, and I spread the cards and letters across the carpet in front of me.

Family friends sent a check for $385. Jerry wasn't one to accept charity, but he acquiesced and wrote back, "I consider myself to be pretty tough—surviving two wars, multiple sclerosis, immigration (Jerry's journey!), and now a loss of beloved daughter. However, when I read your card with the check, I got totally 'unglued' and cried like a baby (Please keep it a secret!) I am a very lucky man to be blessed with such wonderful people as all of you."

Stephanie's student Heidi wrote: "Every time the hairs on my bow flow across the strings on my violin, I can hear her voice. 'Put a little more umph in it, Heidi!' she says. Then she shows me. She isn't here to show me anymore. It hurts."

Melanie's high school friend Joanne Lipman wrote, offering to help get media attention. Stephanie, Melanie, Joanne, and Miriam Simon had played in a string quartet in their teen years. (One of their favorite pieces was Haydn's String Quartet no. 53 in D Major, "The Lark.") Joanne, who went on to become editor in chief at *USA Today* and a chief officer at Gannett, was a journalist with good connections. "I've been thinking non-stop about you and your family since I heard the news," she wrote. "If you think more widespread coverage would do any good, I know lots of people in newspapers and TV."

Jerry took her up on her offer, and in December 1991 a piece ran in the regional section of the *New York Times* entitled "One More Blow to the Heart for Survivor of Nazi Terror." The article told Stephanie's story, including limited details about her emotional teenage years and the "desolate" winters on Martha's Vineyard, which Jerry again blamed for her depression. "I think about Steph every two minutes," Jerry said. "She dominates my life."

★

THAT HOLIDAY SEASON saw a flurry of newspaper articles and prayerful holiday greetings. As my eyes pass over the array of cards and letters on my living room floor, my mother's own handwriting leaps out at me, recognizable before I consciously identify it. "As the mother of three daughters," my mother wrote, "my heart goes out to you and your family upon the disappearance of your daughter Stephanie. Our prayers are that she may be safe and that the new year will see you reunited."

Stephanie's college boyfriend R. J. Vealey and his mother were quoted in an article in the *Charleston Gazette*. R. J. said he and Stephanie had spoken about her problems on Martha's Vineyard. "We've all been at points where you wonder if it's really worth it," he said. "Hopefully, she decided to check out for a while."

His mother, Rosie, added, "I don't think I could hurt any more if it was one of my own. We're all hoping she has amnesia or something and she'll be found. That would be the greatest Christmas present of all."

Tom's mother wrote to Jerry, too. Soon after Stephanie's disappearance, she had a dream. Stephanie, whom she'd never met, appeared to her. "You don't need to worry about this," Stephanie said. "Tom has nothing to do with this." Tom's parents had the same feeling Dee and Molly did: that Stephanie and Tom were a perfect match. Her dream of Stephanie proved it. "I have wanted to write you for some time, but I have not had the words to express our family's complete sadness. It is incredible that people can go from such joy and happiness to utter despair in so short a time," she wrote.

For Tom's family, part of that despair had to do with their utter lack of trust in the police. Over twenty-five years later, they are still indignant—not just about how Tom was treated, but about a more systematic failure on the part of the police, which led to Stephanie's remains going undiscovered for nearly seven years.

From day one, Molly and Dee felt brushed aside. They felt less and less urgency on the part of the police every time they called, even in those first few days. They insisted that Stephanie would never leave her birds. "It's like a mother leaving a baby at home," Molly told the police.

Dee organized her own unofficial search party, and rode her horses through the town's fields and backwoods, hoping the higher vantage point would help. They brought stacks of posters emblazoned with Stephanie's face everywhere they went.

One officer mocked Dee when she begged the sheriff's office to check the fields near Newcastle a week or two after Stephanie went missing. "What, do you think she's lying half dead in a field some-where?" he said.

The worst part was how the cops treated Tom.

Even with the ceaseless support of his family, Tom was wearing down, his sisters could see. The love of his life was missing, probably dead. And the only worldly thing he had to remind him of her was Chubie, who, that fall, had begun laying eggs for the first time in her life.

Tom wrote to Jerry, beginning by saying how much he missed Stephanie and how happy she'd been, and updating Jerry on the cockatiel:

> Chubie seems to be happy and I am glad her egg-laying has stopped. Her latest act is landing on a book's edge I am reading while lying on my sofa. While perched there, she tries to eat the pages so I have to shoo her away or play with her. I am very glad to have her.

About a week after his first letter, Tom sent another, this envelope containing also a clipping from the *Rochester Times-Union*. Sergeant Donald Farrell, the man who accused Tom of murdering Stephanie, had been arrested and charged with third-degree grand larceny, a felony. Tom wrote, "We suspected the quality of the investigators from the beginning and this is pretty strong proof. Maybe it will help in getting the FBI involved."

Tom also sent Jerry a Christmas gift. He'd taken Chubie's three eggs to a Ukrainian folk artist, who decorated them in intricate patterns of gold and black and rich deep red in the traditional Ukrainian *pysanka* Easter egg style.

My mother still has the eggs—each only about an inch long—in a tiny liqueur glass on a shelf in her china cabinet. I never knew until last year that they had come from Stephanie's bird. I have always liked rotating them to follow the details of their designs, holding them with the lightest touch of my fingertips.

★

IN 1992 JERRY increased his reward to $10,000. The *Star-Ledger* newspaper published an article when Stephanie had been missing for just shy of a year. Sergeant Murray told the reporter they hadn't ruled out foul play and were working on the case "every week." "It's like a wound that won't heal," Jerry was quoted as saying. "You sort of get used to it, but it doesn't hurt any less."

Jerry kept paying the private investigator, whose work produced nothing. Jerry and Melanie kept reaching out to the media. Hope fluttered in their hearts at every lead.

In October 1992, several women's bodies were found near the Ontario State Parkway, not far from where Stephanie's checkbook had lain in the dirt. Stephanie's coworkers Kim and Carl Fink wrote to Jerry to say the police suspected the work of a serial killer. "Stephanie's dental records were checked, and ruled out. Stephanie continues to be, very much, on the minds of the police," they wrote.

The women were identified; all had links to drugs or sex work, so it wasn't likely these crimes were connected to Stephanie, anyway. These were the women John White was later suspected of murdering.

Hope was dashed again and again.

Sergeant Connors, the lead detective on Stephanie's case, wanted nothing more than to find her. But soon enough, a new horror caught Connors's attention.

21

ANNETTE ALFEROV WENT to bed the night of April 9, 1992, at around 10:00 P.M., her six-year-old daughter Yvonne sleeping in the next room. Annette awoke from a deep sleep, aware of a misty light shining through the space between her bedroom curtains, to the sound of an intruder in her living room, and wandered out to face a stocky man, about six feet tall and pudgy in the middle, wearing a dark-colored baseball cap and a white hockey mask that completely covered his face.

She had started to ask what he was doing there when he shoved a crowbar across her throat, pushing her into her bedroom and onto her bed. He told her to shut up—he'd only come to take things, he said, and then he handcuffed her.

"What time is it?" the man asked.

"I need my glasses," Annette told him.

He got them for her. It was 2:30 A.M.

"Please don't hurt me," Annette said calmly.

"I won't," he said. "Are you married?"

She lied and said yes, and her husband, a truck driver, would be home around 4:00 A.M. She tried to keep the conversation going, to stall whatever he might have planned. He told her he'd been in the country a few months. He repeated he'd come to steal from her, and it would be fine since she had insurance. "I don't have insurance," she told him.

"What are you, a dumb ditzy bitch?" he said.

"I may be dumb, but I'm not a bitch," she answered.

He asked how many children she had; she lied and said two. "You're a liar," he told her, correcting her. "You have one. What's her name?"

"It's Susan," she lied again.

"I've been watching you," he told her.

She could smell the liquor on his breath as he stripped her bed and covered her head with her own pillowcase. He found pantyhose in her dresser and used it to tie her ankles and hands to the bedposts.

"Why are you doing this?" she asked.

"All women deserve this," he answered, stuffing something black and lacy into her mouth. She spit it out; he sealed her mouth closed with gray duct tape. He asked her if she wanted some "reefer or Jack Daniel's" and he left the room. He returned with a container, found a straw in her kitchen, put it near her mouth, and told her to drink. She recognized the taste of Jack Daniel's.

For the next few hours the man raped her orally, vaginally, and anally. He said the most vulgar things imaginable about her body, made her say she loved what he was making her do, and methodically beat her buttocks with something that "hurt like hell," possibly a Rubbermaid cake mixer from her own kitchen. "All women like this," he told her.

"No, they don't," she said.

"They deserve to get beat," he said.

Sometime later in the haze of her assault, Annette asked what time it was. He told her it was 5:00 A.M. When he was finished, he lay down next to her. "Now I don't know what we're going to do. You've seen my face," he said.

Annette wrote in her statement later that morning that she thought he would kill her. When he mentioned her seeing his face, she said, "He sounded like doom."

She assured him she hadn't seen him. "I promised I wouldn't look, and I didn't," she said. "I want to live. I want to raise my little girl," she pleaded, thinking of Yvonne, sleeping on the other side of her bedroom wall.

"I know what we are going to do," he said. He forced her into the shower, telling her to stay in there and wash herself completely, inside and out. She stayed until the hot water turned freezing cold. The man took the stockings and some of Annette's bedding and put them on a wash cycle in the laundry room. He warned her, in a bizarre moment, "If you don't want me to come back, put a deadbolt on your door and a pole in your window."

He told her not to tell anyone because she'd never catch him, and even if she did, it would be her word against his. He told her to stay in the shower for another ten minutes, and he left. She waited, then grabbed her keys, purse, and daughter, ran to her upstairs neighbor's apartment, and called the police. It was the morning of her thirty-third birthday.

Annette lived directly across the parking lot from Stephanie's apartment. The windows of their bedrooms faced one another. Annette remembered that the week before her assault, she'd come home to find her closet door open, which she found so strange she'd called her mother to ask if she'd been in the apartment.

Now she wondered if the same man had already cased her home before he broke in and raped her. Annette couldn't recall hearing the front door open when her attacker left to get the Jack Daniel's he made her drink. She felt a strange intuition that the man had stashed the alcohol in the utility room before that night.

Six-year-old Yvonne mostly slept through her mother's assault. All she could tell the police was, "I heard Mommy talking to some man, but I couldn't understand what they were saying."

That weekend Connors and Armstrong were back in Poughkeepsie to interview Stephanie's cousin Ivan. They wanted him excluded as a suspect. He signed his statement hours before Annette woke up to find a rapist in her bedroom. When they returned to Greece, the horror of Annette's assault eclipsed everything else in their workload.

Annette drew a crude sketch for the cops of the assailant's mask. She was an intelligent victim who had a good handle on what had been done to her.

The detectives started canvassing the complex, asking the women who lived there what they knew. Four days after Annette's assault, a neighbor named Sheryl told Connors and Armstrong that two former Newcastle Apartments employees had once told her they wanted to "screw" Annette Alferov. Randall Glen and his brother-in-law Ed Laraby had come by Sheryl's apartment several times in a "drunken stupor" and made sexual overtures to her. Laraby bragged about beating his wife, and said that he knew where every single woman in the complex lived and what she did for a living.

Four months earlier, in January 1992, another resident had called to report an unlawful entry. She also mentioned that Laraby, a former maintenance worker at the apartment complex, had been making her uncomfortable by saying sexually suggestive things to her. She wondered if Laraby might have been the man who'd entered her apartment and left before she could see his face. Laraby had been in her apartment on at least two other occasions for "bogus maintenance calls," entering through the laundry room, not the front door of the building, asking her "what kind of sexual activity she liked" and to "take a ride in the truck" with him. She got rid of him both times by saying her boyfriend would be home soon.

The cops looked up Laraby's record. He had been in prison for sexual assault for the majority of his adult life. Every time he was out of jail, he'd raped again. He was known to wear hockey masks during sexual assaults committed in the past. This was all before the sex offender registry was created in New York in 1995, so the women had no way of knowing he was in their midst. Laraby lived less than a mile from all of their apartments, including Stephanie's. In the next two months, there were two more rapes, with similar MOs, in the nearby Monroe County towns of Penfield and Henrietta.

If they could pin the rape of Annette Alferov on him, he'd never get out.

Sergeant Murray put a photo of Laraby on a desk with five others and asked Annette, "Can you identify any of these men?"

"Uh-uh," she answered, shaking her head.

Connors and Armstrong were undeterred. They interviewed Newcastle's resident manager William Shaffer. Shaffer told them Laraby had worked there from January 1991 to July 1991, when he was sacked for insubordination. Laraby had been in Annette's apartment twice to make repairs, and on one of those occasions, Annette was home with Yvonne.

Shaffer told them he'd gotten several complaints about Laraby's behavior from female residents in the few months he'd worked at Newcastle. He directed the police to yet another resident, who told them about the times she had encountered Laraby. He came to fix her furnace and told her, "I'd like to jump into bed with you."

A month later, she awoke from a nap to the sound of someone exiting her apartment; fifteen minutes later, Laraby rang her doorbell and apologized for mistaking her apartment for one where he had a repair to make. The woman had been sleeping naked from the waist down and suspected Laraby was watching her sleep. Most recently, in early July 1991, she met Laraby in the parking lot, where he agreed to help her install a chain lock. Once inside her apartment, he tried to hug and kiss her and said, "I wouldn't mind eating you, licking you all over, satisfying you."

She told him to leave.

In haste, Sergeant Murray put together a confidential criminal intelligence form in the days following the rape. "Ed Laraby is currently on parole for robbery and has an extensive criminal record for violent sexual attacks against women," it began, and then explained that Laraby was often seen driving around in his red Plymouth or riding around on a bicycle. Any after-dark sighting, especially in the vicinity of Newcastle Apartments, was to be reported immediately. The report was not to be mentioned on any police radio, just in case he or any of his friends were tuning in.

There were few clues. The photo lineup was a wash. A rape kit was completed, but Annette had showered. There were a few partial prints on the washing machine. When Murray searched Annette's home, he listened to her answering machine. On it was an obscene message; a male voice asking Annette to pick up. "I want to blow my wad to the sound of your voice," the man said.

When Murray played it for Annette, she recalled that she had received the message only five days earlier, and she seemed sure the man on the tape was the same man who had raped her.

Six days after Annette's rape, Sergeant Murray interviewed another maintenance worker at Newcastle named Rick, trying to ascertain if anyone had information that could point to Laraby more surely. Rick surprised Murray by mentioning not Annette but Stephanie. He'd seen Laraby talking to her, and what's more, Laraby had told Rick he thought Stephanie was "cute" and he "didn't see any men around."

Laraby was also (though no one realized it at the time) the same man whose son with the "active imagination" had said Stephanie had absconded to South Carolina.

★

STARTING IN THE first week of July 1992, the police created a multi-agency surveillance team to track Laraby, including manpower from the Monroe County Sheriff's Office, the Greece Police Department, and the Ogden Police Department. It was a delicate undertaking to track a man who would inevitably assault another woman. If he caught on, they would never get him. But if they weren't glued to him, he would inflict irreparable damage to yet another victim.

They observed Laraby for months, as he moved from his new job at the Genesee Stamp Metal Company to one of the local bars where he'd drink—in violation of his parole—after work with his wife Terry's brother Randall Glen, and then as he'd drive around residential neighborhoods, peering through windows. On July 24, Laraby and Glen picked up a sex worker in Laraby's truck, but then they vanished from the police's sight. The woman soon ran into the street from between two buildings, screaming for help. Sergeant Patrick Crough wrestled Laraby onto the hood of his cruiser and brought him into custody, but had to let him go because he invoked his right to counsel, and because the woman refused to cooperate much more than telling the police Laraby had been a client of hers once before, when he had spanked her with a belt buckle and made her call him "Daddy." The team hadn't witnessed a direct assault, so they had nothing.

But that same night at the station, Laraby's brother-in-law Glen wanted to talk. He told Crough he was terrified of Laraby. Glen said he lived with Laraby because he was afraid Laraby would hurt Glen's sister or nephews.

A couple of years earlier, Laraby had pointed a gun at Glen's head, so Glen implored the police not to tell Laraby he'd talked to them. "Do you think he's a good suspect for the Newcastle rape?" they asked, and Glen replied with a quick "Yes."

Glen offered little more, but he said he wanted to see Laraby back in prison.

The police let Laraby believe they were part of a "hooker detail" trying to cleanse the Rochester area of prostitution. This way, their cover wasn't blown. Indeed, area police were in the midst of a conspicuous undertaking to rid the town of illegal sex work—in part because of the thirteen sex workers' bodies that had been found in the past few years, the ones from the clipping Stephanie's coworker friends had sent Jerry.

The surveillance team waited, knowing Laraby would strike again. A few weeks later, a report came in from the Rochester PD of a young man who was grabbed from behind and dragged along the sidewalk. The victim scratched wildly at the face of his attacker, who ran off. It seemed like Laraby's style and the man's description matched. The cops figured maybe Laraby thought the man was a woman because of his small stature and long blond hair, and bolted when he realized his mistake. Laraby lay low for weeks after that, following his mundane route from work, to a bar, and home.

But on August 14, 1992, eight of the men who had been following Laraby for months—including Patrick Crough, who'd just tangled with Laraby a few weeks before and really wanted this done—watched from a discreet distance as Laraby drove his truck slowly down Monroe Avenue, a main thoroughfare in Rochester. Glen was in the passenger seat. Laraby passed two teenage girls, turned onto a side street, and parked. He appeared on foot a moment later, sauntering down Monroe Avenue, slightly ahead of the girls, later identified as Bethany Swenson and Dawn McCall. He turned toward the girls, continuing to stroll past them, then about-faced and picked up his pace as he closed in on them. The surveillance team was situated in several cars, so they had a panoramic view of the ordeal.

Laraby ran to cover the last few feet between himself and the girls, then struck quickly, wrapping his arm around Bethany's throat in a choke hold, grabbing at her pubic region with the other hand, pulling her toward him with such force that she was lifted off the ground. Dawn spun around and took a swing at Laraby, striking him in the left arm. Bethany managed to wriggle loose from his grasp, and Laraby started running back to his truck.

The officers swooped in from multiple directions, capturing and cuffing Laraby after he turned a corner and neared his truck, where Glen was waiting. As they tossed Laraby into the back of a cruiser, he yelled out desperately, "Shoot me! Just shoot me!"

Bethany hadn't seen his face, but Dawn had, as she turned to hit him. He struggled against Crough, writhing around as he was forced out so Dawn could take a look at him. They asked her to identify him since they'd captured him just out of her sight; they wanted an airtight arrest. As soon as she saw Laraby, she pointed and said with certainty, "That's him. That's the man who attacked Beth."

Laraby refused to reenter the car and was laid facedown on a lawn as he kicked out at the officers. A wagon arrived to transport him, now cuffed at both his wrists and ankles. Once inside, he began to thrash around violently, bashing his face and head into the windows and walls of the vehicle. "Look what you cops did to me!" he cried when the doors were opened. The police photographed his bloodied head before he was removed from the back of the wagon.

The girls had narrowly escaped Laraby's violence; they were relatively unscathed. But Laraby was behind bars again.

According to his rap sheet, Laraby had never killed anyone. His MO was to leave his victims ashamed and alive; it was as though he got off on their debasement. He had humiliated Annette and Sheryl—and they had both been Stephanie's neighbors. Connors could stand in the parking lot outside Annette's house and nearly see into Stephanie's bedroom window. This was a proximity he couldn't ignore.

22

I F CONNORS WANTED to understand Laraby, Glen seemed like a good place to start. He'd been working at Newcastle Apartments since 1988 and was the one who got Laraby his job. His arrest record included burglary, forgery, drunk driving, and disorderly conduct, but no sexual assault or otherwise violent crime. His employers had recommended him for promotions and raises, and it seemed like he was mostly trying to live a straight life. Maybe Connors could get him to turn on Laraby more than he already had.

Glen claimed to have been asleep in the passenger seat the night of Laraby's arrest, and said he knew nothing about what had happened when Laraby attacked Bethany Swenson in Rochester, nor about Annette's assault. But he tipped Connors and Armstrong off to a guy named Wolf Patterson. Wolf, he said, knew something.

Wolf Patterson, a Native American tattoo artist, got to know Laraby when they were in prison together and was scared of breaking his parole, so he talked openly to Connors, admitting he'd tattooed Laraby's inner groin with a rudimentary spider tattoo.

Laraby had come to see Wolf in late April 1992. He told Wolf he was wanted for the rape of a woman in the complex where he used to work, but he wasn't the perp. It was someone else. Laraby told Wolf he "did all kinds of kinky shit to her."

Laraby said the woman had described her assailant's tattoos, so he wanted Wolf to add a tattoo she wouldn't have been able to identify.

Wolf gave him a blank release form, which Laraby returned, dated December 13, 1991, over four months before Annette's assault, so it would look like the tattoo was older than it was. "I realized he was trying to cover himself," Wolf said.

He agreed to keep the form on file, and he brought Connors a copy. He even drew a sketch of the spider dangling from its web, including the broken and double lines he'd intentionally scratched onto Laraby's groin to make the tattoo look old and amateur. The web, he said, was the size of a fifty-cent piece.

All it took was a search warrant for the detectives to compel Laraby, in jail now, to drop his pants and show them the spider. It was an exact replica of the one Wolf had drawn. The search warrant also got them some of Laraby's saliva and blood to run DNA tests to try to solve Annette's rape case. But the rape kit didn't show anyone's DNA other than hers, and Wolf's hunch that Laraby was the rapist wasn't enough.

Still, Laraby was off the streets, awaiting trial for the sexual assault of Bethany Swenson.

In January 1994 Laraby was found guilty, easily, of first-degree sexual abuse and attempted third-degree assault. The jurors, Assistant District Attorney Ken Hyland says, were "creeped out" by Laraby.

At the sentencing in June, reported the *Rochester Democrat and Chronicle*, Hyland said, "The defendant is a predator. Instead of hunting animals, he hunts women." The sentiment was echoed by Judge Eugene Bergin, who said to Laraby, after comparing him to the velociraptors in the movie *Jurassic Park*, "It's my opinion, were it not for the intervention of the officers who had been stalking you, you would have killed that young lady."

Laraby is the only criminal Hyland has ever truly been afraid of. "He was someone I thought could come after me if he got out. Everything about him was scary," he says. "I believe there are people that are born bad—others who suffered. I don't know which he is. He was amoral, asocial, and had no conscience."

Laraby's appointed defense attorney, Mike Schiano, describes Laraby as "the scariest guy" he has ever represented. He says Judge Bergin, who previously encountered Laraby in court in 1981, broke protocol to praise the jury after they delivered the verdict. "You have no idea who this is. He's got a rap sheet you wouldn't believe," he told them.

Edward Laraby was sentenced to twenty-five to life, and wasn't up for parole until 2017. Connors at least now had a captive suspect, and he wasn't going anywhere. Connors would regroup, think of some way to get Laraby talking.

While Connors always kept Tom, Geoff, Chris Mosher, and my step-father in mind as potential suspects, after Annette Alferov was raped in April 1992 and Laraby arrested that August, his attention refocused on Laraby.

Connors wanted nothing but to find Stephanie. At this point, he felt sure he would not find her alive, and he suspected Laraby might know where to find her body.

PART III

Corruption and a Cold Case

23

F AST FORWARD. IT'S 2015, and I'm in Rochester for the first time. At 7:30 A.M. in a downtown Rochester café, Todd Baxter, former Greece police chief, drinks a mug of black coffee while I stir honey into an almond milk latte. Jazz plays in the background.

It's two days after my meeting with DA Sandra Doorley, and my mind is swirling with too many facts. All I know is that Todd Baxter was chief when Stan Chizuk and Mike Ives picked up speed on Stephanie's case, which had been cold for nearly a decade, since Dave Connors retired in 2000.

"I love cops and police work," Baxter says, when I ask what attracted him to his field. "Guys go out there and lay it on the line for complete strangers; you can't pay people enough. You do that because you want to do it, because it's your calling."

Baxter is gregarious, charismatic, always smiling. Only about ten years older than me, he is both venerable and youthful, with a handsome cleft chin and unassuming wire-rimmed glasses. He's easy to talk to. I ask how he became chief in Greece.

"I was a police officer in Rochester, watching all the chaos and corruption in Greece and laughing about it. The job opened, I love to lead, and it was a great opportunity to do something different. I wanted to see if I could change a corrupt department. I went out there for four years, lost a lot of hair," he jokes.

I want to understand not only why Baxter had recommitted to Stephanie's case two decades after she disappeared, thirteen years after her body was found (and ten after Connors's retirement), but also what had caused the case to languish in the first place. And Baxter straight-up tells me, "The corruption stifled everything." Otherwise, he says, maybe Stephanie's case could have been solved years earlier.

I have no idea what he means by "all the chaos and corruption," but I keep listening as he tells me how he took over for Chief Merritt Rahn, who somehow wound up behind bars. I just listen.

In a police department like that, Baxter says, "You don't go above and beyond, you don't take risks. Maybe you don't make all the arrests you should, just the ones you have to. You do what you have to do, not what you need to do."

★

BACK IN 1991, when Sergeant Dave Connors was leading the investigation into Stephanie's disappearance, there was no internet. The information he was able to collect on the case came from direct interviews and was logged using a pad and a pencil. And the information he gathered was, in retrospect, nothing short of commendable.

Connors knew all the facts; his all-caps penmanship and meticulous note-taking show a sense of deliberation, a depth of thought and attention, a disinclination to leap to conclusions. When Stephanie's body was found in 1998, Connors told the *Democrat and Chronicle* that he was "obsessed" with the case.

When Todd Baxter became chief in 2010, and Stan Chizuk and Mike Ives picked up Stephanie's case, that obsession was the bedrock of their investigation. Stan Chizuk calls Connors "the custodian of that case."

Their entire search was based on a foundation found in cardboard boxes and stacks of paper, a huge pool of information provided by Connors, who became a sort of third partner in a time-bending collaboration. On one end, there was Dave Connors and his scrupulous investigative work—work that had been surrounded by corruption and damaged morale and productivity, corruption that, as Todd Baxter suggests, surely stalled the resolution to Stephanie's case. But his labor would provide an invaluable asset pool for the men at the other end of the eighteen-year timeline. Stan Chizuk and Mike Ives, meanwhile, possessed innovative interviewing techniques and an amiability that allowed them to knit themselves close to a suspect. And in those in-between years lay the story of a police department that crumbled to pieces.

It was a twist of fate that led to the reopening of Stephanie's case. The downfall of the corrupt chief Merritt Rahn—the chief Connors worked under for most of his career—brought in Todd Baxter. It is only because Merritt Rahn was fired and imprisoned that Stan Chizuk and Mike Ives were assigned Stephanie's case at all.

★

WHENEVER MY FOCUS lands on Rahn and the corruption of the Greece PD, it feels like I am abandoning Stephanie. But these tracks inevitably cross. These seemingly disparate narratives are ultimately inextricable from one another.

Those cops were the people who were supposed to help find her killer. The more I research that police department, the more clear it is how the political push and pull created an environment of mistrust and tension that existed long before Merritt Rahn was even in Greece, as far back as the 1970s, or before. The Greece Police Department was a classic good old boys' network, filled with fecklessness, nepotism, and self-serving men.

Greece was a place where honorable cops like Connors had to keep their heads down to get anything done. Connors was stoic by any definition, but if it were me trying to solve rapes, murders, and disappearances under such discord, it would grind me down. I've worked in schools with leaders that lacked vision or integrity, and I know the wearing down of vigor that happens when you have to ignore the system you're in so you can accomplish what you want in spite of it. That was the swamp in which Stephanie died, and in which her case went cold.

The more I learn about the Greece PD, and the repeated instances of abuses of power there, found in the archives of the *Democrat and Chronicle*, the more Todd Baxter's words make sense: "The corruption stifled everything."

24

I N JULY 1992, ONE year after Stephanie's disappearance, three months after Annette Alferov was raped, Merritt Rahn was appointed "safety commissioner" of Greece after the commissioner at the time unexpectedly retired. This position existed on and off in Greece, usually when someone with clout wanted the current police chief under greater scrutiny.

Rahn was slim and dark-haired, had a squeaky-clean record, and was lauded in Rochester for his work fighting organized crime. He was seen as "a straight shooter."

Soon, Chief Gerald Phelan, who had been accused of threatening and harassing his subordinates, suddenly retired without fanfare, and all claims against him were dropped.

Rahn was appointed chief of police.

Accusations flew at Rahn fast. Only two months after he became chief, the Democrats in Ogden accused him of forging his wife's and brother's signatures on a Conservative Party petition there.

Rahn's hitherto spotless record saved him. Because he was respected, the Ogden town court saw no reason to make a mountain out of a molehill, and agreed not to try him, on the condition that no more charges were brought upon him for six months. "I learned a heck of a lesson," Rahn said, promising to be on the up-and-up.

For a while, it was Greece as usual—burglaries, DUIs, another murder-suicide, accusations of discrimination because the force employed no officers of color, a massive child pornography bust.

But "normal" in Greece also included more alleged small-scale corruption on the part of Merritt Rahn. He'd purchased one hundred commemorative police badges, raising the suspicion of his detractors in the Rochester Police Department, who requested a state investigation into the matter. There was talk, too, of Rahn coming to the aid of friends and acquaintances who'd received speeding or DUI tickets, getting involved in cleaning up crime scenes, making certain charges disappear for friends of his kids, things like that.

In August 1995 the town board suspended Rahn. In September he was arraigned on charges of coercion, falsifying records, petit larceny, misconduct, and criminal solicitation. He was accused of removing items from the property office—computers, calculators, radios—threatening an officer, and asking another officer to get a friend's kid out of a speeding ticket. He faced a maximum sentence of fifteen years in jail.

That same summer, on June 27, 1995, there was another murder in Greece that would in time, like Stephanie's case, go cold. Timothy Milgate's wife took their two daughters, along with Timothy's mother, to see the movie *Pocahontas*. When they returned home, they found Timothy dead in a pool of his own blood in the front hall; he'd been shot twice and stabbed multiple times. His family held fundraisers and offered rewards for information, conscripted the help of State Attorney General Dennis Vacco, and highlighted his case on *Crime Stoppers*. Still, there was never much of a lead in any direction. After all, while police were investigating Milgate's case, they were also distracted by the accusations and charges against their own chief—and probably worrying about their own hides.

In the *Democrat and Chronicle*, Jack Rittler, the president of the Greece Neighborhood Association, questioned "the effectiveness of a department when it's under such a cloud."

And Tony Narr, an expert on the dynamics between communities and their police, lent his take: "A department takes on an aura of whatever's being accused. Those things can tug at the morale of a department unmercifully."

★

THE PEOPLE OF Greece wanted answers about Rahn—and they wanted them right away. And some of those people were people who loved Stephanie Kupchynsky. Among them was Tom Redmond's sister Dee, who wrote an article entitled "What Happened to Stephanie?" lambasting town leaders and the cops. She was furious that the constant disorder might be distracting from finding Stephanie. She hoped the *Democrat and Chronicle* would publish the article. "The problems we experienced with the police department stem from leadership," she wrote. "Our town supervisor needs to make this his highest priority. Especially now, our new chief of police needs to organize the department, keeping all officers informed of current, unresolved situations each shift, every day. A more competent department would have acknowledged that Stephanie had already been missing for over twenty-four hours when they were first notified."

The *Democrat and Chronicle* faxed Dee's letter to the GPD for comment. Appalled, Connors wrote back a three-page defense, going point by point through Dee's article.

Dee said that Tom and Stephanie were engaged; they weren't. Dee said the GPD told Tom they had to wait at least twenty-four hours before completing a missing persons report; in actuality, the report was begun on August 3, 1991, at 12:01 A.M., only hours after Tom's arrival in Greece. Dee wrote that the GPD didn't take their concerns seriously; Connors countered that in 1991, there were 348 missing persons reports in Greece, in all of which family members were concerned about foul play. Connors explained that the things he'd learned about Stephanie early on—that she'd stopped taking her meds, that she'd behaved erratically and impulsively in the past—led him, in fact, to doubt foul play. Dee claimed that both the Greece and Brockport cops tried to slough off the responsibility of looking into Chris Mosher, who found Stephanie's checkbooks; Connors protested that both departments worked in tandem to eliminate him as a person of interest. And perhaps most egregiously to Connors, Dee said that there was actually a *prior* rape in the complex that was mishandled; if she meant the rape of Annette Alferov, that had occurred seven months *after* Stephanie's disappearance. "The 'previous rape,'" Connors wrote, "NEVER HAPPENED."

The paper decided not to publish Dee's letter, and her chance to use Rahn's scandal as a platform to bring more attention to Stephanie's case was lost.

★

THIS WAS ALL going down in the first few years Stephanie was missing, at the same time that Connors was following leads and trailing suspects. Though Connors was adamant in his response to Dee's letter, perhaps, as Todd Baxter has implied, he didn't feel as free, supported, creative, or assertive as he might in different circumstances.

In October 1995 a county grand jury refused to indict Rahn for the felony charges and dropped some of the misdemeanors. The chaos continued, and Connors did his best to push on.

25

E ARLY IN 1996, Connors tracked down a prison buddy of Ed Laraby
and Wolf Patterson's named Steve Smith. Smith told him that back
in jail, Laraby had said repulsive things about women; whether he was
reminiscing or fantasizing wasn't clear. During sex, Laraby said, he'd
"step on their backs" to cause pain, and "slit their throats because it
made everything tighter," Smith reported.

He said Laraby told him a good place to get rid of a gun was in the
swamps near Lakeshore Drive. The last time Smith had spoken to Laraby
was in July 1992, a few weeks before he attacked Bethany Swenson. He
told Smith he was in so much debt, he might as well be back in prison.
But nothing Smith reported from his conversations with Laraby involved
Stephanie.

Later in 1996, acting pro se, Laraby started plotting again from prison.
He hoped to have his conviction overturned based on the fact that he
was "intoxicated" at the time he assaulted Bethany Swenson, and had
suffered from drug and alcohol addiction for years. Terry Laraby and
Randall Glen wrote affidavits swearing to intimate knowledge of Laraby's
problems with drugs and booze—and said that if their testimonies had
been used in Laraby's trial, he might have been acquitted.

"I have known my husband for twenty years," Terry had written. "I
have witnessed my husband's continued and frequent intoxication and
abuse of drugs. I have witnessed my husband's insomnia, severe depression, eating disorder, blackouts, and hallucinations."

Glen wrote that on the day Laraby assaulted Bethany, he had drunk at least seven beers and five shots of Jack Daniel's and snorted a lot of coke, and his reason for parking the truck in Rochester, around the corner from where he attacked Bethany, was to go buy more. Glen vowed again that he knew nothing about the assault.

Laraby's defense attorney Mike Schiano, after seeing the forms and forwarding them to the Greece Police Department, didn't think the affidavits were of much help, especially because they seemed to have been "probably written by Laraby," anyway, as he told the police. Glen's statement wasn't even signed.

In the end, Laraby's work was for naught. He stayed behind bars.

★

MERRITT RAHN, MEANWHILE, managed to avoid going to jail. A Rochester City Court judge dismissed the last three charges against him in May 1996. The town board still had to decide on the civil charges. In June, it returned Rahn to the payroll. A *Democrat and Chronicle* opinion piece read, "If the town board agrees to reinstate ousted police chief Merritt Rahn, it will be headed for a train wreck in a tunnel darkened by secrecy."

On July 12, 1996, Merritt Rahn was indeed reinstated as police chief—with a $144,000 settlement. The *Democrat and Chronicle* eventually got their hands on a copy of the agreement made between the town and Rahn, which an editor called "a slick piece of revisionist history that essentially says the Rahn debacle never happened."

After Rahn got his job back, Todd Baxter says, "He was really empowered. He came back with a vengeance. Anybody that turned against him, internal or external, got wiped off the face of the earth."

Timothy Milgate's father, like Tom's sister Dee, was irate about the department's pandemonium. He demanded that his son's case be given more attention. He was appalled that over a half million dollars had been spent on Rahn's case, when six months after his son's murder, Greece police had told his family they couldn't afford the overtime to work on Timothy's case anymore. "Where on Earth do politics and personal squabbling take precedence over solving a murder?" Robert Milgate asked in a letter to the *Democrat and Chronicle* in May 1997.

Stephanie's family could have asked the same, but Jerry mostly stayed out of Connors's investigation. Melanie put her head down and went on with life, raising her three small kids and playing in the Chicago Symphony Orchestra. Jerry got together with my mother and was a newlywed at sixty-eight. He wanted to teach his students in his basement studio and sit on the deck of their new house listening to Beethoven, not keep going in circles looking for his daughter. Life had drawn and quartered him, and he lived in two realities—in one, he was a gentle retiree with a new wife, and in the other, a bereft and despairing father.

Stan Chizuk was hired in 1997, after spending his rookie years in the upstate New York towns of Caledonia and Canandaigua. For the next ten years or so, Stan says, Rahn wasn't much more than "an absentee landlord" in "a toxic environment."

Rahn may have never directly blocked the investigation, but the drama around Rahn certainly didn't help it move forward. The danger to the department was not a bullet to the head; it was more like a slow-acting venom.

26

O N MAY 6, 1997, Connors received a phone call from Greg Livadas, a reporter from the *Democrat and Chronicle*. He couldn't let go of Stephanie's story, and he knew the cops were eyeing Edward Laraby, so he had taken it upon himself to pen a letter to Laraby, appealing to his sense of justice and closure. Livadas, like many others, had never stopped wondering whether Stephanie was alive or dead. He hoped Laraby would help him bring an end to the story and tell him where Stephanie was. Laraby responded in April, ready to haggle. He wrote:

> If I were to agree to talk to you, it would be under certain conditions. I would not allow any recording devices—video or audio. I would not allow any notes to be taken. You would have to come during regular visiting hours, as a regular visitor, and come alone.
>
> Before this can occur, I would require a show of good faith on your part. I have been experiencing some difficulties obtaining some photographs from my arrest and booking from August 14, 1992. I would like you to obtain these for me. A very simple request.

Laraby's letter brimmed with hubris, as though he were not a man serving twenty-five to life but one on equal footing with the police. He wanted the photos the cops had taken that night of him in "a bloody and battered condition" after he'd thrown himself around the police van. Livadas didn't write back. But he thought Connors should know about it.

Connors was still hounding the prison for any nuggets of information they could offer about Laraby. He came into contact, through prison counselors, with the guy in the next cell at Auburn Correctional Facility, Alvin Pereira. Pereira was willing to talk if Connors came in plain clothes.

So, on May 22, 1997, Connors made the drive to Auburn. He was announced to Pereira as a "first time visitor"—a code phrase he'd passed on to Pereira beforehand. Pereira's girlfriend and her two teenage daughters visited that day, too, and sat nearby drinking sodas and playing rummy while Connors sat across from Pereira to pick his brain about Stephanie.

"Laraby never mentioned her until he got a letter from that reporter," Pereira said. "He told me all about the father wanting help finding her, about the photos he tried to get from the reporter."

Connors pressed him for more. "All Laraby ever said was, 'I know about what happened, but I wasn't directly involved.' I didn't believe him."

Laraby and Pereira had both been pretty sure Livadas's letter was a ploy, a setup by the cops. Connors assured Pereira that he hadn't been involved, but now that Laraby and Livadas had been in touch, he wanted to see if he could push the conversation forward.

"What I really need," Connors said, leveling with Pereira, "is to know where she is."

"If I figure that out and testify," Pereira replied, "you gotta get me out of Auburn."

"I can't guarantee that," Connors told him, "but I'll see what I can do."

After a few months, Connors checked back in with Pereira, but he had nothing new. So he contacted Livadas again, who agreed to reply to Laraby and see what he could dredge up. At the beginning of September, Livadas wrote to Laraby:

> I was not able to obtain the photographs you mentioned through several channels. It sounds like you're pursuing some sort of legal action. I'd suggest you have your attorney subpoena them.

I hope this doesn't dissuade you from wanting to meet with me. As far as you requiring a "show of good faith," all I can say is that I'm offering you the opportunity to tell your side of the Stephanie Kupchynsky story for the first time. I'm assuming that since you are apparently considering meeting with me, you feel you have something to share with my readers.

My intent has not changed. I'd like very much to write the story that brings closure to one of the most fascinating missing person cases I've ever covered. That closure will only be possible if the remains of Stephanie Kupchynsky are located and returned to her family.

Laraby never wrote back. Instead he decided to write to my stepfather.

★

THE ENVELOPE WAS addressed to Jerry care of the "East Brunswick Public School System"; someone had forwarded it to him in the house he'd moved into with my mother, the house on whose back deck I had stood as they got married.

My mother recalls the day Jerry got that letter. "I remember coming home from work and Jerry just sitting at the table, not quite with it. He said, 'I've just got this letter—look at it.' And I looked at the brown envelope and I said, 'Jerry, this looks like it comes from a prison or something.'"

My mother sat next to him, and together they read what Laraby had written:

I don't know if you are aware of who I am, but a reporter from the Rochester, New York Democrat and Chronicle, Greg Livadas, has contacted me with regard to a 1991 incident.

Mr. Livadas has sent me some of his articles in which he quotes you as saying, "If I have to devote the rest of my life to this, I will have to," and that "my greatest fear is that this will just be swept under the rug and forgotten."

It's safe to say Mr. Livadas has his own agenda, that being to write a story in which the end result will glorify his record as an investigative reporter, therefore he can hardly be trusted.

The same can be said for the District Attorney's Office in that area, they also have an agenda of their own. Unfortunately, you and yours are not a part of that agenda. You are from New Jersey and your other concerned family members are from Illinois. Your not voters in their area and you have no political clout with them, therefore they will not make concessions to resolve your dilemma. Your greatest fear may come to be reality.

I would consider an open dialogue with your representative for the possible resolution to your dilemma, but like everything else there must be a few basic conditions.

Until a mutually agreed upon time you may not contact the media, you may not contact any law enforcement agencies, which include District Attorney's and private investigators. Any deception will terminate any dialogue.

Your representative may only be a bonafide member of the clergy. If you agree to these terms a dialogue will be opened.

May the peace and grace of God be with you.

This letter was saturated with the same hubris as all of Laraby's letters, complete with a saccharine and incongruous prayerful closing.

My mother and my stepfather sat in stunned silence. Though Laraby had strategically failed to mention Stephanie by name, there was no denying the inference that they'd just read a letter from Stephanie's likely murderer.

Jerry had been without his daughter for six and a half years. Now the main person of interest in her case was offering information. He couldn't miss this chance. He had to be both deliberate and prudent with his next move.

His friend connected Jerry with her pastor, Kenneth Haupt, of Christ Memorial Church (the church visible from our backyard), who met with my mom and Jerry and agreed to correspond with Laraby. Jerry wrote back, saying he accepted Laraby's terms. Pastor Haupt reached out to Laraby, who wanted to make sure any communication between them would be guarded by the confessional privilege.

Haupt was in touch with a lawyer and planning a visit to the Auburn Correctional Facility when, in April 1998, fate intervened: Chris Weber and Justin Whipple found a skull in a small stream just outside Holley, New York.

27

M Y MOTHER'S HEART jumped at the sudden loud sound of a telephone ringing in the dark. She fumbled for the receiver, whispering "Hello?" so Jerry wouldn't wake up. His Parkinson's was getting worse; he was more feeble than he'd been even seven months before, when she married him.

Melanie asked my mom if she'd heard yet.

"What are you talking about?"

The police had found Stephanie's body, Melanie told my mom.

A newspaper reporter had called Melanie for commentary. That was how she first learned, in April 1998, almost seven years after she'd received the call that her sister was missing, that her sister was definitely dead.

"We were in a daze," my mother says. I press her for details: How did Jerry react? What did he feel? But that's all she can say. *A daze.*

★

AFTER GRADUATING FROM Rutgers University in May of that same year, I moved my things back to my mom and Jerry's house for the summer. I was up late one night packing for a trip through Belgium, France, and Italy. Everybody else—my mother, stepfather, and sisters—was asleep, and the lights were out throughout the house, except the one over the sink, where I was washing a few dishes before I turned in. With my back to the open kitchen, I suddenly felt a kind of trembling that seemed to

Front page of the Democrat and Chronicle, *April 17, 1998*

float into the room from behind my right shoulder, near the entrance to the dining room. I breathed and steadied myself. Nervous about what I might actually see if I looked, I stared straight forward, avoiding my own reflection in the kitchen window above the sink. It was something like the feeling when you know someone is watching you, or like the subtle change in air pressure when another person walks into the room. An imperceptible hum of energy. But more just a sudden shift in my own being. I wondered if it could be Stephanie. "She's only curious," I told myself.

I stopped what I was doing and, with deliberate calm, padded up the stairs to my room. As my foot hit the plush carpet of the second floor, the unsettling weight of another person's presence fell away like a heavy cloak. My breathing eased. I went to sleep.

The next morning, I asked my mother if Stephanie had been around the house.

"Absolutely," she said. "She's been all over. One day I was vacuuming the bedroom, and she was in there. I said, 'Steph, I know you want to be near your dad, but this is my house, too. You can't come in our bedroom.' And poof, she's never been upstairs since then."

For me, the strange energy seemed to originate in the dining room, which adjoined the kitchen. What I didn't know at the time was that Jerry had been collecting condolence cards there, displayed on a table, and arranged around the same photo of Stephanie that had been next to the wedding cake the summer before. My mother said Jerry had been spending a lot of time in that room, looking at the photo, reading the cards, and not talking.

★

AFTER SHE'D BEEN gone for so long, suddenly it felt as if Stephanie was everywhere. Not just a spirit visiting my mother's house, but back in the media, too. There was a storm of news articles right after her bones were discovered; people in New Jersey and near Rochester remembered her name and her face.

The AP published a short update in the *New York Times* on April 17, saying, "Early on, her father, Jerry Kupchynsky, of East Brunswick, N.J., appealed for his daughter's return through newspapers and television shows, holding out the slim hope that she had amnesia or had intentionally disappeared. In recent years, however, he said he had come to accept the likelihood that she was killed."

Greg Livadas wrote a front-page piece for the April 17 *Democrat and Chronicle*, naming Laraby as the main person of interest and containing a timeline of his run-ins with the law. It includes a photo of Jerry and my mom sitting on their couch, holding a photo of Stephanie.

In an article by Sue Epstein on the same day in New Jersey's *Star Ledger*, Jerry says, "I've been bleeding emotionally for the whole time. Even though the little spark of hope I maintained all this time that she was alive was extinguished, I'm relieved."

The next day, Janine Kava wrote in the *Democrat and Chronicle*, "The discovery of Stephanie Kupchynsky's remains could trigger old memories and revive clues once dismissed as irrelevant, bringing new life to the investigation that has mystified investigators for 6 ½ years."

Yet there was still no motive, no confession, no solution.

On April 19, *Democrat and Chronicle* opinion writer Mark Hare wrote an op-ed entitled "Maybe her bones will prod Stephanie's killer to come forward." In it, he wondered if Stephanie's killer would step into the light. "I don't believe in monsters," he wrote. "Even the worst offenses are committed by people capable of doing the right thing."

28

D AVID CONNORS KNEW that no one was going to suddenly have a change of heart and simply volunteer a confession. He had to get to work.

Connors was on his own as the case kicked into high gear. His investigative partners had all retired: Don Farrell in 1992 (soon after the scandalous arrest for larceny about which Tom had written to Jerry), Mike Murray in 1997, and Dennis Armstrong—who'd kept a photo of Stephanie on his desk next to his own children's photos for years—in March 1998, just a month before Stephanie's bones were found.

Connors didn't even have much support from Stephanie's own father and sister. The emotional toll of the discovery of Stephanie's body was so intense that both Jerry and Melanie pulled back from efforts to figure out what had happened to her. Now that his daughter had been found, Jerry wanted nothing more to do with Laraby. Pastor Haupt wrote one last time to Laraby on May 7: "Mr. Kupchynsky sees no further value in my coming to visit you, now that Stephanie's body has been discovered."

Jerry and Melanie mourned their loss and moved forward; Connors dove back into the details of the case that required further investigation.

Remembering that there'd been a discrepancy in the mileage on Stephanie's car, Connors replicated her last day's known journey, starting at Jiffy Lube (where the odometer reading had been so recently noted), then going to Maxine's place and the airport—but adding in a side trip to Hurd Road, where Stephanie's body had lain. It was eighty-six miles total, exactly the difference between the mileage Jiffy Lube had recorded and the mileage on the Nissan's odometer when it was found at the airport. Someone had used Stephanie's own car to get her to that creek.

Next, Connors reinterviewed two witnesses who had separately reported seeing a woman in a red sedan—like Stephanie's—near the town of Holley, around the time of Stephanie's disappearance. One said the woman in the car had looked as though her hands were bound; the other said she looked scared. Under hypnosis, the two witnesses now provided more information about the people in the car; one was even able to produce the first three numbers of the license plate: 445. Connors ran the plate number and followed the lead to an elderly couple in Kenmore. But it was a dead end; the couple assured him that no young person had ever driven their car, nor had it been stolen or borrowed. The plates didn't match up to any person of interest in the case, either—not Geoff, not Tom, not Laraby.

Connors pressed on, consulting with a meteorologist: the night of July 31, 1991, was partly cloudy with a waning full moon, which would make it bright enough to find the way from the road to the creek without a flashlight.

He combed through over thirty pages of records from the airport parking lot, looking for any glitch.

And he reinterviewed a cabdriver who in 1991 had reported picking up a strange fare leaving the long-term parking lot the night of July 31. The cabdriver, too, was put under hypnosis and remembered an unac-companied and "agitated" man without luggage in a torn white T-shirt asking for a ride that night. He was able to describe in detail the house where the man was dropped off. But when Connors searched the area the driver reported, he could find no house matching the description.

Meanwhile, Stephanie's left tibia was found in the stream, ten days after Chris and Justin's initial discovery. Missing, according to the medical examiner's report, were her mandible, sternum, left ulna and radius, sacrum, right tibia, both patellae and fibulae, assorted vertebrae and ribs, and numerous bones of her hands and feet. There were mud deposits on some of her bones and black sooty marks caused by fungus. That vibrant girl who loved her birds was a list of bones.

The coroner studied the jigsaw puzzle of Stephanie's skeleton for months, and in July 1998, the autopsy was finally finished. Stephanie's death was officially ruled a homicide; cause of death, unknown.

Late at night, lying in bed at my mom's house that summer, I found myself wondering how my stepsister had died.

Connors touched base with Stephanie's high school friends Sharon Case and Janine Orlando, her Martha's Vineyard friend Nancy Dole, and her Greece friends Paula deFranco and Maxine Ellison, the woman who'd seen Stephanie last when they went out for ice cream. They were shattered all over again by the confirmation of their friend's murder, but as much as they wanted justice for Stephanie, they had nothing new to add to Connors's investigation.

Connors called Tom Redmond, who by then had moved to Painted Post, New York, in the Finger Lakes region, with a new girlfriend he'd later marry. He only had one new story to share with Connors. He remembered now that on the Friday or Saturday after he'd found Stephanie's apartment empty, three maintenance workers had passed him in the hallway of the building—one with a "sly grin."

Even though Connors didn't consider Geoff Fletcher to be a prime suspect in Stephanie's death, he had questions, and tracked Geoff down; he was living in California. Geoff was agreeable and cooperative. Stephanie was never actively suicidal, but she was close to the edge, Geoff told Connors. He said he didn't realize what an effect the abortion would have on her and did have some regrets.

Connors again tracked down Chris Mosher, the young man who had found Stephanie's checkbook on the side of the road. He'd been in and out of trouble since 1991; jailed once for another bad check, he had his parole revoked. He'd been arrested three days after Stephanie's bones were found. Connors drove over to the Orleans County Sheriff's Office to meet with Chris, who was back in jail awaiting a trial for grand larceny. In his report, Connors wrote, "When challenged on the veracity of his prior account of how he came into possession of the victim's checks, Mosher began to cry. No new information developed."

★

Case timeline

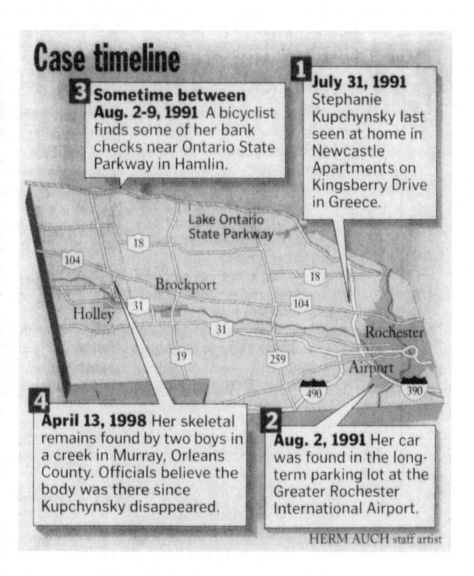

3 **Sometime between Aug. 2-9, 1991** A bicyclist finds some of her bank checks near Ontario State Parkway in Hamlin.

1 **July 31, 1991** Stephanie Kupchynsky last seen at home in Newcastle Apartments on Kingsberry Drive in Greece.

Lake Ontario State Parkway

18

104

Brockport

18

Holley

31

104

31

Rochester

19

259

Airport

490

390

4 **April 13, 1998** Her skeletal remains found by two boys in a creek in Murray, Orleans County. Officials believe the body was there since Kupchynsky disappeared.

2 **Aug. 2, 1991** Her car was found in the long-term parking lot at the Greater Rochester International Airport.

HERM AUCH staff artist

CONNORS'S NOTES FILL more than two hundred pages. Most of them center on Edward Laraby.

Laraby's now ex-wife Terry resisted Connors's requests. TV stations had been calling her home; her younger son Josh, who was only nine, picked up once or twice. "Because I have a child, I am trying to forget the bullshit of being married to Edward," she said to Connors. "He is my past, not my present. I don't want to know he ever existed. He brought me nothing but heartache."

When Connors pressed further, Terry erupted. "I don't know nothing! Everything I thought was true I'm beginning to wonder about."

"About what happened?" Connors asked.

"About anything in my entire marriage to the man," Terry said. In the end, she was no help.

He reached back out to Laraby's boss William Shaffer. Shaffer said he'd cried his eyes out when he saw the news of the discovery of Stephanie's body. But he couldn't add anything.

Connors got in touch with a man who had worked at Newcastle Apartments and knew Laraby. "I told Shaffer he'd be sorry he hired that guy," he said.

Next, Connors tracked down a friend of Laraby's tattoo artist Wolf Patterson whom they called "Wildman." He said that on August 1, 1991— the day after Stephanie's disappearance—Laraby had come looking for Wolf at his mother-in-law's house. Wildman said Laraby went inside for ten minutes, then left. Shortly after, Wolf left, too.

Connors considered this. Maybe Laraby was looking for help covering his crimes of the night before. Maybe Wolf had helped bring Stephanie's lifeless body to that shallow stream where she stayed, ravaged by the seasons, for seven years. He had, after all, once tattooed Laraby, helping him escape blame for the rape of Annette Alferov by allowing him to pre-date the paperwork for the tattoo to before the attack.

Connors was starting to feel he had a foothold on the case. He tracked Wolf down to an address in Missouri and called the state police there to try to get him in for an interview.

While he waited for word from them, he set about finding Wolf's ex-wife Sally. He called Sally's mom—who told him Laraby was often at her house, talking with Wildman and Wolf—and got Sally's number in Oklahoma, where she was living with her new in-laws. "I don't know anything about this!" Sally said. "Laraby probably would've asked Wolf for help, and he probably would've helped him. But I don't know anything else! Wolf is long gone."

Connors also appealed to the FBI for help. In 1985, in Quantico, Virginia, the Violent Criminal Apprehension Program (VICAP) was created. It was a database of homicides—both solved and unsolved—sexual assaults, and cases of both missing and unidentified persons where foul play was suspected. The driving thought behind its creation was that it would enable disparate police departments to draw similarities among cases, streamlining their work and making it easier to identify criminals and their patterns.

Connors applied to have Stephanie's case entered into the VICAP database. The FBI agreed to do so.

He also learned that two other Greece officers had registered another murder with VICAP—the 1995 murder of Timothy Milgate. The detectives on the case had worked for three years without much to go on. When they sent their case to the FBI, Agent Tom Doktor from the Buffalo FBI office wrote back, inviting them to discuss it with the Behavioral Science Unit of the FBI Academy. Connors saw an opportunity—a chance for fresh, enthusiastic, critical eyes on loan from the FBI. He arranged to travel down to Quantico and present Stephanie's case alongside Timothy's, and to visit Jerry and my mother in New Jersey on his way back to Greece.

Connors put together a thorough packet of information for Agent Doktor, including the details surrounding Stephanie's disappearance and the whole circuitous narrative of Laraby's arrest and incarceration, culminating in the letter he wrote to my stepfather earlier that year. Connors was befuddled as to why Laraby had, until Stephanie was found, continued to offer information about the location of Stephanie's remains. He wrote,

> The question here is why would Laraby make these efforts to have the body discovered.

Our thoughts are that he is doing so in order to place the blame on someone else. That this "someone else" also knew the location due to their participation in the crime with Laraby or from what they'd learned from him. Otherwise, if Laraby committed the crime by himself; if he never told anyone about it; and the body hadn't been discovered after almost seven years, why would he want to facilitate its discovery now?

While we have been told that he enjoys the media hoopla he causes, he hasn't taken advantage of any of the offers that have come to him in prison from the media for interviews.

Connors said his main purpose in meeting with the Behavioral Science Unit was to ascertain ways of approaching Laraby's closest acquaintances, most of whom were afraid of him. In particular, Connors was preparing for the conversation with Patterson he hoped to soon have.

The two items at the top of his to-do list: interviewing Wolf again—and obtaining a hair sample from Stephanie's family, in case her DNA was needed for any reason.

★

ON HIS DRIVE back north from D.C. to Greece, Connors stopped in East Brunswick, New Jersey. My mother answered the door and invited him inside, where he proceeded to fill them in on what he knew. Jerry handed over Laraby's letter, and Connors said he would like a sample of Stephanie's DNA.

He had hair and other debris that had been vacuumed from Stephanie's car back in 1991, but he had no "control hair"—hair that was definitely Stephanie's—to provide to a lab. Nothing like this had been collected from Stephanie's apartment in 1991—why, I'm not sure. Perhaps because at that early point the police thought Stephanie would return, and it wasn't yet considered a crime scene; or perhaps it was because the technology had improved so much since 1991. Either way, long before 1998, when her case officially became a homicide, someone else had moved into that apartment, and nothing there would be useful. He hoped my mother could help.

"We cleaned out Stephanie's room before we moved; Melanie has everything," my mother told Connors. "I'll call and see if she can find anything—a hairbrush, maybe."

"A hairbrush with hair in it would be perfect," Connors said.

After Connors left, my mother called Melanie to ask her to go into her garage, take down the boxes filled with Stephanie's things, and look for a hairbrush.

To my mother's surprise, Melanie refused. She insisted the cops would have found hair in her car if they could. None of this would bring her sister back.

"What if it stops someone else from having the same fate?" my mother pressed. But Melanie was adamant.

"I felt sorry for her," my mom says. "I don't understand how someone could not care enough to help someone else avoid the same fate. That's beyond me—she didn't know for sure who did it; how do you know it wasn't someone who would come after her family? She had a difficult childhood, between her mother's illness and her overbearing grand-mother and being trotted out for performances all the time. But I could never understand why she wouldn't try to find some DNA. I brought it up gently a couple of times, but her answer was always the same. Once they found her sister, that was it."

So Connors had to move forward without DNA that was surely Stephanie's. What's more, the hairs they had found in the car were soon deemed "poor candidates" for DNA typing, anyway.

My mother and I were nervous that they had the wrong guy somehow, that whoever had killed Stephanie was still free and dangerous. If the police had narrowed their sights too soon, had possibly settled on Laraby merely because of his criminal history and proximity, regardless of the total dearth of real evidence, it was certainly possible.

While we had a nagging fear Laraby might not be the one who killed Stephanie, Connors worked to prove he was. He wrote to Laraby in prison, asking him to open his mind to a conversation. He got an answer from Bob Napier, the defense attorney Laraby retained after Stephanie's body was discovered: "Absolutely not."

In Missouri, police at last learned that Wolf was working for a traveling carnival. In August, Wolf called to say he'd gotten married and had settled in Abilene, Texas. Connors arranged a tentative deal for Wolf with ADA Ken Hyland, who wrote a letter promising immunity to Wolf if he'd helped to cover up the crime—but not if he was involved in the homicide itself—and was forthcoming with any information that would lead to an arrest.

Connors traveled to Texas exactly one year after Stephanie's bones were found. Wolf repeated the same story his prison buddy Wildman had told Connors of the day Laraby came to Sally's mother's house, but he added nothing new.

Connors kept toiling at Stephanie's case, but he was in the twilight of his career. He retired in the spring of 2000, two years after Stephanie's remains were recovered. He maintained his belief that Laraby was guilty.

Connors closed his report, written on June 10, 1999—his last I can find—with two words.

"Nothing further."

29

A ZARIA GREEN WAS born eight years after Connors's retirement, in the early-morning hours of June 7, 2008. The night of Azaria's birth would spark the complete deterioration of the Greece Police Department and set off a chain of events that resulted, ultimately, in the reopening of Stephanie's case.

A few hours earlier, Alexis Sharp, only twenty-five weeks pregnant, and her fiancé, Teran Green, had visited Alexis's mother in Rochester. As they made their way home to Greece on Route 390, the car stalled, and Alexis guided it over to the left edge of the road. Teran turned on the hazard lights, and Alexis took out her phone to call for help.

At that moment, officer Nicholas Joseph was speeding down the same highway in his brother David's Ford SUV. Security footage from Spenders Bar in Rochester proved he'd spent the night downing drinks, and he wasn't wearing his seat belt when he plowed into the back of Alexis's car. Her car careened into another lane, where a second car slammed into it. The "black box" in the SUV later showed that Joseph had been going eighty miles per hour.

Alexis, bruised and battered, was rushed to the hospital with shoulder, back, and head injuries. The trauma kick-started premature labor, and Alexis underwent an emergency C-section. Azaria barely survived her own birth. She weighed less than three pounds when she took her first breaths. Her brain was bleeding, and she had significant respiratory and liver problems. She spent the first weeks of her life in the NICU suffering from head injuries, and she continued to struggle with physical and mental impairments, according to the charges brought against the town by her grandmother in 2009. She was lucky to be alive.

Officer Joseph hit his head on the windshield so hard that the cops who came to the scene later found blood on the glass. In photos taken hours later, Joseph's face is cut up and bruised, his right eye swollen shut. For some reason, Joseph exited his car and began walking down the highway, winding up at his home in Parma some ten miles away. He was "dazed and confused," he claimed, and didn't know how he got home.

The report issued by Greece police said Joseph didn't call the police department for at least eight hours. Joseph said he called fellow officer Gary Pignato and Chief Rahn a few hours after the crash, but Rahn said he didn't know for three days that there were any other injuries besides Joseph's.

State police took over the investigation, in which Rahn swore there was "no cover-up." Allegations that Joseph was snorting cocaine that night surfaced when blood found on his car's airbag tested positive for cocaine—and matched his DNA. A bartender from Spenders testified she'd served him five drinks in one hour; the crash occurred fifteen minutes after he left the bar.

Joseph was indicted and charged with aggravated vehicular assault, second-degree assault, operating a motor vehicle while impaired by alcohol and cocaine, leaving the scene of an accident, criminal possession of a controlled substance, and perjury. He faced, if convicted, a sentence ranging from probation to twenty-six years behind bars.

Sandra Doorley, then ADA for Monroe County, was the prosecutor. Joseph was found guilty on all counts, fired, and sentenced to three to seven years in jail. But the investigation began to uncover a pattern of unethical, if not illegal, behavior in the department that went well beyond Joseph.

When officers arrived at the scene of the crash that night, they took neither photos nor measurements of the scene, and they failed to impound the SUV, even though its driver had fled. Rahn, still as slender as he'd been in 1995, but now with a shock of white hair and a thick mustache, said he was "upset" that certain protocols had been ignored, and town supervisor John Auberger said the case was "an embarrass-ment." The county's new DA, Democrat Mike Green, soon opened an investigation into the ordeal.

In the comment section of a local online news forum, furious Greece townsfolk spun theories. Many thought Rahn, whose scandals thirteen years earlier suddenly seemed very fresh again, was to blame.

"The entire Greece Police Department is corrupted," one wrote. "They allowed the rats to get away with this disgraceful conduct. Merritt Rahn, your time is over."

"If I lived in Greece, I would be terrified to call 911 and get a GPD officer," said a third.

One wordsmith even wrote a limerick:

In Greece, there's a police chief named Merritt,
Whose words his lieutenants would parrot,
Then along came a cop
Whose car wouldn't stop.
Whose mess will this be to inherit?

When DA Green began his inquiry, he said, "On the one end, you could have just plain old sloppy work. And on the other end of the spectrum, you could have a cover-up."

Joseph's buddy Gary Pignato was under fire, too. Within months of Joseph's wreck, a woman came forward saying Pignato had coerced her into sex after showing up at her boyfriend's house when she was drunk on vodka, in violation of her probation—based on a petit larceny of under $50. Pignato told her she could "avoid going to jail" if she met him later that night, she said. She did, and the two went to his house and had sex. Pignato confirmed they had sex, but swore it was consensual. He never completed a report about her drinking, though, which, pros-ecutors argued, proved that the alleged sex-for-silence swap was real.

Twelve more women came forward with similar stories about Pignato, whom online critics dubbed "PIGnato." One woman said she was emboldened after the initial allegations; her story was almost the same. Pignato shadowed her in his cop car as she drove home and asked for her number. Then, without ringing her bell or knocking, he breezed into her home a few days later while she sat on her couch smoking pot. He said she could lose custody of her kids, but he "would take care of it" if she had sex with him. She met Pignato the next night, fearing the loss of her children. "He was demeaning," she testified.

Pignato was found guilty on the felony charge of receiving a bribe and the lesser misdemeanors of coercion and misconduct. He was fired, then sentenced for up to six years. He later pled guilty to misdemeanors stemming from the second woman's charges, and got two more years running concurrently with the first sentence.

The consensus in Greece was one of shaken faith. Alexis Sharp and her fiancé each sued the town, contending that the police had covered up the wreck to protect Joseph, and that he should have never been hired anyway, based on his "checkered past."

Town supervisor John Auberger swore he'd get to the bottom of the lies and corruption. He hired a retired state cop, Joseph Loszynski, to work in tandem with the DA and run an in-depth inquisition into the department. "There will not be a rock unturned," Loszynski assured the people of Greece.

In late April the DA's office subpoenaed records related to Nick Joseph's accident.

That Saturday, Merritt Rahn showed up at headquarters with two other officers on what was their usual day off. The noisy grind of a paper shredder caught the attention of officers on duty; they called in the state police, who arrived to find scores of official-looking documents reduced to confetti. On Sunday the town board held an emergency meeting and voted 4–0 to suspend the trio.

By May, the volume of paperwork related to the investigation was so immense the town hired six more retired officers to aid Loszynski. Finally, Loszynski announced that he and his team had over three hundred leads on the misconduct of Rahn and other officers.

Rahn's attorney declared the town's charges amounted to a "witch hunt" by the town supervisor, John Auberger; Loszynski wasn't even qualified to make the charges, the attorney said. Folks online pointed fingers Auberger's way, too, suggesting that he'd only hired Loszynski to cover his own culpability. "It's time for Rahn to take down Auberger," someone wrote. "Let's end this and save the taxpayers millions. C'mon, Merritt, speak up now."

The DA's office soon charged Rahn with eight felonies and three misdemeanors. Rahn turned himself in on the felony charge of "offering a false instrument for filing" in June 2009, then resigned from his job that October. Auberger sent a letter to the residents of Greece: "Merritt Rahn," he declared, "will never again wear the uniform of the Greece Police Department."

30

IN JANUARY 2010, GREECE was once more without a police chief. Loszynski's squad took on the task of finding a new one. Out of eleven candidates, and after 435 hours of legwork, one man shone brightest: Rochester police captain Todd Baxter.

Baxter's friends from the Rochester force offered glowing testaments. "He will never ask you to do something he's not willing to do himself," said one sergeant. "He is truly a leader," his chief said. "It's in his posture, his demeanor, his way of seeing and thinking about things."

Baxter was sworn in as chief of the Greece PD in February. "Trust does not come from mere words," Baxter said, promising to get into gear and regain the town's confidence right away. "Trust comes from action."

When Baxter took his post in Greece, he tells me that day we meet for coffee, the department brimmed with mistrust, and the townsfolk were skeptical of the people tasked with their protection. "I had to change three things," Baxter says, counting on his fingers. "The cops, the culture of the cops, and the community."

He had to rebuild the tattered department itself. There were seventy officers in a department that called for ninety-four, two bosses where twelve were needed. He hired, promoted, and shuffled people.

He had to change the environment. "They hated each other. How do you fix that?" he asks me rhetorically.

He says it was "a constant push, push, push," answering his own question. "There's an honor and a nobility in policing, so I built on that. [I told them], 'You seventy are here for a reason. You could've left or transferred, but you didn't. We're gonna build upon you. I'm going to have to trust you.'"

Baxter won over many of them. "I can never say enough good about him," says Stan Chizuk. "He is the best chief that department had to this day."

The third and most challenging thing Baxter needed to repair was the community's trust. "They hated the police department," Baxter says. Within his first month, Baxter was put to the test by a triple homicide. He appeared, on no sleep, at a community outreach meeting the day after the murders. This prompted sparks of hope for their new chief among the townsfolk.

Wherever Baxter saw an opportunity for repair, he took it. He had to get the town to first trust him, and then trust the department, or the chasm between the police and the people would be permanent. One of his first moves was to refresh focus on three unsolved cases: the Holiday Inn fire of 1978, Stephanie's murder in 1991, and the murder of Timothy Milgate in 1995. Even if he couldn't close the cases, he would at least show the townsfolk that he would try everything in his power to do so. He'd put his best detectives on the cases, he'd give them all the support they needed, and he'd chase every lead he could until he was absolutely sure none were left.

His goal was not necessarily to find answers once and for all, but to hone more finely the approach to the cold cases and make sure the department did the job right, now that Rahn, the chief who might very well have impaired the entire department, was gone for good.

★

AT 2:38 A.M. on November 26, 1978, the ninety-one-room Holiday Inn was packed; three busloads of Canadians had come to Greece for a few days to do some Christmas shopping, and guests from two nearby Saturday-morning weddings were staying the night.

Harold "Bud" Phillips of the Greece fire department was driving home from running an errand when he saw flames shooting through the roof of the motel. He called it in, then rushed to the scene, attempting to rescue as many people as possible. "There was nothing but screaming," he recounted.

The fire leaped up from a first-floor stairwell and shot across the roof. There was so much smoke, firefighters couldn't see whether guests were in their rooms through the windows. People who couldn't escape through the motel's doors broke through windows and jumped. There were no smoke alarms or sprinklers.

One hundred and twenty-five firefighters showed up from six different departments. A fire chief from Albion, who helped about ten people escape from the second floor, told the press, "I've never seen fire move as fast as it did there."

Ten people lost their lives, and thirty-four more were injured. Three days later, an arson expert from New York City confirmed the worst: the fire had been set intentionally. The ten deaths became homicides.

Suspicion clouded around none other than the firefighter who first called in the fire, Harold Phillips. He was also the last person to inspect the Holiday Inn. But he maintained his innocence. And decades later, he became the town's fire chief.

When Baxter looked at the old files concerning the Holiday Inn fire, brought to him in three disorganized boxes, it was clear to him the investigation was "not done to standard by any means."

He assigned a task force to reexamine all the evidence, attention to the case surged, and eventually the police announced they had a suspect. Many assumed it was "Torch," the nickname townsfolk often used for Phillips.

Ultimately, glitches arose. There just wasn't enough hard evidence to indict Phillips. There were rumors that a second suspect had confessed. But even though the case remained unsolved, Baxter's commitment to the case invigorated some of the town's residents. He had shown he cared and had sincere ambitions of correcting the department's past shortcomings. Others still felt he could have done more. But mostly everyone agreed he was an improvement over Rahn and Rahn's predecessors.

Baxter's aims now clear, he promised officers vast leeway and financial support on two other cold cases: the murders of Timothy Milgate and Stephanie Kupchynsky.

★

AFTER BAXTER TOOK the reins, Stan Chizuk's partner Mike Ives—with Sandra Doorley's help—requested a DNA test on evidence found in the hallway where Timothy Milgate's body had been found. The evidence had never been tested.

Although Timothy's sister Debbie never gave up hope that her brother's murder could be solved, she knew the drama around Rahn had taken a toll on the efficacy of the GPD. "The system has kind of failed me in some ways," Debbie told the *Greece Post* in July 2010 after Baxter's arrival, "but I'm very confident in who's working on Tim's case."

Debbie was sure she'd have an answer soon. She had faith in Baxter and his new team.

But sadly, the DNA test yielded nothing, and the following year, Debbie was diagnosed with leukemia. She lost her fight against cancer—and her search for her brother's murderer—in October 2014. But again, as with the Holiday Inn case, the town saw that Todd Baxter meant business.

Timothy Milgate's murder would never be solved. Stephanie Kupchynsky's still might; Stan Chizuk and Mike Ives had taken it up with renewed passion, and they were working hard. The people of Greece waited, their hopes raised, to see whether, in this instance, Baxter's GPD could deliver real results. And they waited to see if Merritt Rahn would finally be brought to justice.

31

A S BAXTER'S STAR rose, Rahn's reputation declined.
ADA Sandra Doorley opened Rahn's trial two months after Baxter claimed his job. It was heavily publicized, and more came out about Joseph and Pignato's pasts. It turned out that Pignato had been fired from the Rochester Police Department before being hired in Greece. He had unsuccessfully sued the department, claiming that his firing was due to "reverse racism," evening the score after a black officer had been fired a few months before. Pignato's record of misconduct had continued from Rochester into his next job in Wayne County, where he'd almost had charges brought against him for inappropriate treatment of women. And Joseph, in his stint with the Rochester PD, had once been found guilty of violating a man's civil rights by wrongful arrest. More recently, someone had called 911 after witnessing Joseph speeding and weaving on the highway.

People wondered how the two had ever been hired in Greece. Pignato and Joseph started pointing fingers everywhere else, in a game of corrupt telephone.

Sergeant Robert Trowbridge, one of the men on the team that arrested Edward Laraby in the Bethany Swenson case, was suspended from the force, and admitted to falsifying Pignato's background check. The background check included fake letters from two former Rochester police chiefs and one from Rochester mayor Bob Duffy, who later said "there was no way [he] would ever give a positive recommendation" for Pignato.

Trowbridge said he'd fudged the background check at Rahn's request. Rahn, though, said it was Auberger's choice to hire Pignato, so he figured it was a "fait accompli," and he had to make it happen. Auberger swore he knew nothing about the cooked-up background check and thought it was legit.

Trowbridge, who'd been covering for his chief before, now wanted to come clean. Rahn had told him he wanted a positive report on Pignato, so Trowbridge and Pignato worked together to fabricate the quotes in it. Rahn had told him not to call Mayor Duffy, Trowbridge said.

The prosecution presented a similar narrative regarding Nick Joseph, claiming that Rahn knew the extent of Joseph's infractions the night Joseph almost killed Alexis Sharp and baby Azaria. Worse, he'd purposefully tried to obscure the evidence, telling Joseph on the phone that morning to wait until the drugs were out of his system before going to the hospital. Protocols had been broken, the defense argued, because of inaccurate information about the accident from Rahn's subordinates

In April 2010, Rahn was found guilty on seven counts. On the felony charge of offering a false instrument for filing—that is, Pignato's falsified background check: guilty. On the three felony charges related to stalling Joseph's investigation—hindering a prosecution, tampering with public records, and falsifying business records: guilty. On three misdemeanor charges of official misconduct and falsely reporting an incident: guilty. Five other charges were dismissed. His wife, Marilyn, wept when the verdict was announced. "This is so unfair," she said. "The criminal justice system stinks."

"You were sworn to set the moral and ethical tone for your department," judge Francis Affronti said at Rahn's sentencing, where he gave Rahn one and a half to six years in prison. "The example was one rather of deceit and favoritism and abuse of power." Sandra Doorley called it "a corruption that cannot be tolerated."

Some Greece residents see Rahn as a fall guy for Auberger. Baxter calls him a "tyrant." The truth might lie somewhere in between.

By the time Loszynski and his team were finished, the price tag for the investigation had reached $930,000. In total, eight officers resigned or retired, including Rahn and Trowbridge. In his report of his findings, Loszynski concluded that the corruption ran so deep that he "wondered how the department ever functioned."

The Greece PD, despite a remaining core of solid, honest officers, was in shambles when Todd Baxter took his oath during that hectic spring. The same day Rahn was convicted, Baxter promoted sixteen officers in Greece—men and women he said were loyal and hard-working—to a newly created leadership team. "We're moving forward like a rocket ship," he said.

★

I IMAGINE THERE to be variations on this archetypal trifecta of upstanding cops—the hard-nosed Dave Connors, the politically savvy Todd Baxter, the protective teddy bear Stan Chizuk—all over the country, just as we can surmise that there are Nick Josephs and Gary Pignatos everywhere, too, endangering innocent people and taking advantage of vulnerable ones. Joseph and Pignato just happened to get caught.

I think of the woman Pignato coerced into sex, who must have felt disenfranchised or powerless, who believed that acquiescing to his intimidation was her only avenue; of the many others whose safety or peace of mind he violated; of baby Azaria, born before she should have been, fighting for her life because Joseph came careening down a highway blasted on coke and liquor—and I can't fathom why no one tried harder to intercede.

I remember again Baxter's words when we met for coffee in Rochester: "The corruption stifled everything."

And what impact might these decades of corruption have had on the investigation into Stephanie's disappearance and murder?

"Maybe the administration wouldn't give these guys"—Connors and his team—"any freedom" to really investigate with independence, Baxter says. If they had, he continues, "Maybe you could've had Stephanie's killer long before."

What if Nick Joseph and Gary Pignato had never been hired? What if those women had never faced the trauma of Pignato's behavior? What if Timothy Milgate's murder had been solved before his sister Debbie died?

And I ask one more what-if for Jerry, who died without real closure to the greatest loss of his life, a tragedy that consumed the last eighteen years of his life. *What if?* I wonder, and I remember sitting by Jerry's deathbed, watching his eyes search the ceiling of his hospice room as he muttered "місячне світло," the Ukrainian word for moonlight.

PART IV

Hunters and Prey

32

WHAT FILTERED DOWN to me as a teenager was that the main person of interest in Stephanie's case was a man with a spotty past who was on parole when he was hired as a maintenance worker in her apartment complex. All I knew was that he had been arrested for sexually assaulting a girl my age on the street in Rochester.

Sandra's CD expands the picture for me. When Ed Laraby was released from Attica after an eight-year sentence for robbery, on January 18, 1991, Stephanie had been teaching strings in Greece for just under five months. She'd made friends and was seeing a new therapist. Life was brighter for her.

But Laraby's options were bleak. His brother-in-law Randall Glen had a gig as a maintenance worker at the Newcastle apartment complex. Glen talked to his boss, William Shaffer, and Laraby was hired on January 23 for $6.50 an hour, after lying on his application. Laraby answered the question "Have you ever been convicted of any crime?" with one word: "No." I suppose Shaffer either didn't look into or didn't care about Laraby's past.

Maintenance workers at Newcastle were on call during appointed shifts to respond to tenants' needs. They were given a set of master keys to enter apartments, so they could make repairs when someone wasn't home.

On January 25, Laraby signed a form agreeing to return his keys at the end of each shift, so accusations couldn't be leveled at the crew in case of a break-in. It was a formality, really; the keys were the type anyone could make copies of at a hardware store for a few cents. And in fact each guy held on to a set of keys, only returning them if he quit or was fired. The job was a piece of cake. Mostly, Laraby made quick fixes to leaky toilets, cleaned out clogged drains, tightened valves in washing machines, and changed light bulbs.

Nine times in the months between January and July, Stephanie Kupchynsky filled out a residence service request slip. Seven of those slips were signed by Laraby or Glen. Twice, Stephanie had been home to sign the form. Laraby completed both of those repairs; he stayed at least an hour each time. Also in those six months, Laraby made two repairs in Annette Alferov's apartment, across the parking lot.

By the first week of July, Laraby was getting under his boss's skin. One morning, according to the disciplinary report Shaffer wrote, he heard the raised voices of Laraby and the maintenance superintendent, Willie, outside his office. Shaffer went out to investigate and saw Laraby standing by a workbench, glaring at Willie.

"I suggest you get back to work!" Willie said.

"I don't give a fuck about this job, and you're not going to tell me what to do!" Laraby said.

"That type of language and that type of attitude will not be tolerated as long as you're an employee at Newcastle," Shaffer said, only then realizing that Laraby was clenching a screwdriver in his hand.

Laraby waved the screwdriver in Shaffer's face, taunting him. "Well, I don't particularly care for your fucking attitude, either."

Shaffer took a few steps back. Speaking to Willie but keeping his eyes on Laraby, he said, "I suggest you send this man home for the day, until he can calm down and talk in a rational manner."

But Laraby's hostility only intensified over the next few weeks as he grumbled about finding a new job. On the morning of July 22, as Willie was filling in time sheets, Laraby griped again, "When I get my new job, you won't have to worry about me."

"I don't want to hear the bull today, Laraby," Willie said.

Laraby stared at him. "OK, I'll take a sick day."

"I don't care what you do. You're responsible for your own actions," Willie said, and Laraby walked out.

But once again, instead of firing him, Willie gave him another chance. When Laraby showed up for work on Tuesday, Willie told him if he brought a doctor's note for Monday, they could forget about the incident.

But Laraby was indignant. "If I have to get a sick slip for Monday, I'll get one for Tuesday, Wednesday, and Thursday."

Willie told him that if he did that, he shouldn't come back at all.

Laraby stormed out. He didn't show up Tuesday, Wednesday, or Thursday. On Friday, he came back with a sick slip for Monday. "Did you mean what you said about not coming back?" he asked Willie.

"Yes, I did," Willie said—and Laraby was jobless again.

It was July 26. Five days later, Stephanie took Maxine and her kids out for ice cream, stopped at the Tops market, went home, called her dad, and was never seen again.

★

NINE MONTHS LATER, in the early morning of April 10, 1992, Annette Alferov was brutally raped in her home.

Two and a half weeks after that, on April 29, Laraby tried to check himself into rehab at Park Ridge Hospital, telling the intake counselor he'd been drunk and high anywhere from twice a week to every day since he was eighteen, even getting drunk on homemade wine in jail; that he'd been snorting coke since his release; and that he sometimes took his son's Ritalin if there was nothing else around. He told the counselor that life wasn't worth living—he often fantasized about suicide, and it was getting worse lately because of some "remorse over fucked up things." He said he'd most recently considered suicide on April 12, two days after Annette was raped.

Four months later, in August 1992, the cops caught Laraby as he grabbed Bethany Swenson by her crotch so hard she was lifted off her feet, right on Monroe Avenue. His short bout of turbulent freedom was over.

33

F ROM NEWSPAPERS AND files, I piece together the narrative of Laraby's adult life up to the point he was hired at Newcastle Apartments. Whatever Sandra's CD can't tell me, I find in Laraby's many cameo appearances in the *Democrat and Chronicle*.

By the time he turned eighteen on February 20, 1971, Ed Laraby had been jostled among many homes. At the time, his legal address was that of his stepfather Harold, who had married his mother Alice soon after Ed's birth and given him his last name. He had lived with Harold before, during middle school. This I know from an article published May 7, 1967, entitled "Six Rabbits Rescued When Fire Hits Shed." Fourteen-year-old Ed was babysitting his three younger half siblings when their shed, which housed twenty-five pet rabbits, "raised as a sort of family hobby," caught on fire. The article says that Ed "managed to save six rabbits . . . but couldn't save 19 of the pets." I feel a pang of pity for the tender teenager Laraby might have been, until it occurs to me to wonder: How did the fire start in the first place?

On August 24, 1972, six months after his nineteenth birthday, Laraby enlisted in the army. On his enlistment papers, Laraby answered "Yes" when asked if he had ever been arrested—for driving without a license. He said he had spent fifteen days in jail, the first of his many imprisonments.

Laraby also wrote in his enlistment form that he was in a car accident when he was sixteen and suffered facial injuries that landed him at the Genesee Hospital. How severe the injuries were, he didn't say, but they were bad enough that he lost some bottom teeth and began wearing a dental plate.

When Laraby arrived at Fort Dix in central New Jersey for basic training, Stephanie was about to start third grade in East Brunswick, less than an hour's drive away.

Laraby's tenure in the army was short. After fewer than five days at Fort Dix, he fled.

Later, when asked why he'd run away, Laraby wrote, "I was a kid who never had any discipline in his 19 years of existence. When I got to the induction barracks at Fort Dix and ran into all that discipline, I panicked and took off."

On September 28, the US Army declared Laraby a deserter. Ten days earlier, he had been arrested for assault in Canada. His second prison stay was a seven-month stint in Ontario, where his AWOL status was discovered.

On May 7, 1973, officers drove Laraby across the five yawning arches of the Peace Bridge, which stretches across the Niagara River from Fort Erie, Ontario, to Buffalo, New York. He was apprehended there by FBI agents, who locked him up in the Erie County jail, and then the stockade in Fort Campbell, Kentucky.

Commanding lieutenant Arthur Shemwell agreed that Laraby should be discharged "for the good of the service." When interviewed, Shemwell wrote, "Laraby went to great lengths to show what a tough hoodlum he is. He described nine months in a Canadian jail for assault, during which time, he became a heroin addict. He described 'street life' and considerable prison experience. PV1 Laraby, regardless of the precise truth of his tales, is a very short-sighted individual, who ought to be discharged immediately."

Laraby was discharged, "under conditions other than honorable," on June 8, 1973, and he moved to an apartment in Rochester, near his stepfather.

On October 19, a little more than four months later, a man picked up a fifteen-year-old hitchhiker in Perinton and brought her to a nearby railroad station in his van. There he cut her clothes off, beating her with a belt when she struggled, bound her with a pair of socks, raped her, and left her there bound, gagged, and blindfolded, with her glasses replaced, useless, on her face over the blindfold.

On November 12, a man with a similar description picked up a seventeen-year-old in Brighton, drove her to Cobb's Hill Park, and raped her.

By the end of the week, Laraby was arrested and charged with both rapes.

One year later, on October 25, 1974, Laraby pled guilty to one of the rapes; in exchange for the plea, charges of first-degree sodomy and possession of a weapon were dismissed. He was sentenced to six and a half to twenty-five years. Judge Hyman Maas, in response to hearing of Laraby's troubled, unstable youth, said "Nothing in the whole story would justify what was done that night."

★

BEHIND BARS, LARABY studied law books and became a "jailhouse lawyer"—the inmate who tries to find a legal loophole and get his sentence reversed. In 1976 he filed an appeal, claiming that his sentence was "harsh and excessive." The appeal was denied. He followed two years later with a detailed application for a hearing, claiming that there were several instances of incompetence on his lawyer's part. This time the judge, Donald Mark, granted a trial, noting, "This may be one of those cases where the defendant has developed a belated insight into how his attorney should have represented him. . . . Nevertheless, [he] is entitled to an evidentiary hearing."

Waiting for trial, Laraby worked to clean up his image from inside Attica's walls. He earned his high school equivalency diploma in 1979, was on the dean's list after his first semester at Genesee Community College, and took a course in sheet metal fabricating technology.

Next, he appealed to have his dishonorable discharge upgraded to an honorable one, so that he would have an easier time reentering society and the workforce. Ten letters of recommendation from various friends and family were sent to the Veterans Outreach Center to support his review, describing him with words like *diligent, responsible, well-liked, respectable,* and *level-headed.* The letters, all following the same template and looking as if they had been typed on the same typewriter, claimed he was a decent, upstanding citizen who was making sincere efforts to straighten out and start a new life with his wife, Terry, whom he'd married in 1975 in what must have been a jailhouse ceremony, one year into his first sentence. Even Terry's mother wrote to say Laraby was "trying to better himself to make a good life for [her] daughter."

The army denied the upgrade.

He joined Attica's Seventh Step Foundation, a rehab group based on the seventh step of twelve-step programs, which urges addicts to embrace the pursuit of humility. He became the group's public relations director, and he started writing advice columns for the *Golden Times*, a local newspaper for senior citizens.

His columns were meant to arm senior citizens with safeguards and insights that would help them avoid becoming victims of crime. In one, he recommends good locks for windows and doors: "Remember, the burglar tries to gain entrance into your home as quickly and as quietly as he can. The harder 'YOU' make it for them and the longer it takes them increases the chance that someone will hear or see them. So get tough, senior citizens, and use our tips wisely."

In another, he covers robberies and purse-snatching, advising readers to stay calm if they are robbed. In an almost perfect description of himself, Laraby writes, "The amateur robber is usually a teenager, and more likely than not, he is a vetran [sic] from a broken home, who has no respect or moral convictions. This in itself makes him a very dangerous person."

The day of his trial arrived. Laraby's new defense attorney argued in court that his original attorney had failed to interview Laraby's alibi witnesses—three people who had stories to explain where he'd been on the nights of the rapes.

It worked. Judge Donald Mark, ruling that Laraby's "right to an effective lawyer" had been denied, overturned Laraby's conviction. He was free again on March 21, 1980, reunited with his wife, Terry, who was soon pregnant with their first son.

Three months and one day later, he struck again. A seventeen-year-old girl agreed to get into Laraby's car with him. But Laraby pulled a knife, shoved it against her throat, and, as with his other teenage victims seven years earlier, forced her to perform sodomy. The girl, too scared to tell the truth, told police she'd gone out for breakfast with Laraby before the incident. The lie would cost her.

Laraby was freed on $10,000 bail, and his arraignment for the assault was scheduled for July 23. He didn't show. Someone dropped a tip saying he'd been packing his bags two days earlier, so Judge Eugene Bergin issued a warrant for his arrest.

Border patrol officers in Rolla, North Dakota, were surprised to see a stranger attempting to cross into Canada. At the time, the population of the town was 1,458, so Laraby stood out. Running his name through the national teletype, they discovered Bergin's warrant and arrested Laraby on the spot.

Monroe County DA Charles Siragusa told the *Democrat and Chronicle* that Laraby's mistake was absconding to such an isolated place. "He could have walked across the Peace Bridge in Niagara Falls on Sunday afternoon and no one would have stopped him," Siragusa said.

He was extradited and returned to Rochester on August 6. At his trial in February 1981, Laraby admitted to binding the girl's hands and threatening her with a knife. He pled guilty to first-degree sexual abuse, but because of the victim's lie about the alleged breakfast (which meant, I suppose, that her rape wasn't so bad?), he was offered a plea deal: a maximum of seven years.

Laraby's lawyer had another idea. Laraby would volunteer to be administered twice-weekly shots of Depo-Provera, which, though more commonly used as a contraceptive, was being pioneered by doctors at the time as a treatment for sexual predators. (This treatment, which reduces testosterone significantly, would come to be known as "chemical castration.") This would be better for society, his lawyer said, since a jail sentence wouldn't curb his base impulses.

But Judge Bergin knew Laraby was just trying to stay out of jail. Bergin sentenced Laraby to two and a half to seven years in prison, commenting that "if he was sincere about his desire to rehabilitate himself with this drug, he certainly could do it when he gets out." He added that Laraby had committed crimes other than sexual assault, and that given his previous attempted flight, he was not likely to show up for his treatments. Laraby was back behind bars by mid-April.

In retrospect, the Depo-Provera might have been the better option. Laraby was released after only one month, the five and a half years he'd spent in Attica having been applied to this sentence. He was out again on May 18. Of course he didn't pursue the Depo-Provera treatment.

He kept his head down for over two years.

★

IN JULY 1983 A young housewife took her bike out for an afternoon ride along the Barge Canal, one of upstate New York's meandering waterways. A man wielding a knife leaped out from behind some bushes and raped her.

On October 10, in four separate incidents, someone in a demented-looking Halloween mask meant to look like the wrinkled face of an old man jumped out from the shrubbery along the canal. A nineteen-year-old girl on a bike was robbed of $6. Another teenager ran away from him, and a third jumped into the canal and swam to safety. Then, farther down the towpath, the man encountered a mother and her teenage daughter. He seized the girl, pressing a blade to her throat, and demanded that the mother give him whatever she had. She gave him her car keys and told him where her car was parked. With a pair of blue socks, the man bound the mother and daughter's wrists, and he stole the woman's pocketbook, containing credit cards and cash, before driving the car to a nearby canal access road and dumping it.

For months there were no leads as to the identity of the masked man. Detective Gerald Barker, who was assigned to the cases, mentioned his frustration to his old pal Burton Verhay, a retired detective. Verhay grew pensive while his friend vented about the case.

"There's something about those socks . . ." Verhay said. Famous for his steel-trap memory, he recalled a serial rapist from a decade before with a similar MO—Edward Laraby.

By mid-February 1984 Laraby was in the Monroe County jail, charged with robbery, larceny, and forgery. That October, Laraby pled guilty to two robbery charges and was sentenced to four to eight years.

"If it were in my power," judge Donald Wisner said, "you would not be released after eight years. You have a real sickness."

Laraby was thirty-two. He had spent most of the last decade in prison and was headed back to Attica. He kept a low profile this time. He and Terry had a second son in 1989, likely conceived in what's known at Attica as a "trailer visit," when family members can spend up to forty-four hours in a two-room trailer within prison walls—part of the Family Reunion Program, created by the Department of Corrections after the 1971 Attica riots.

He wasn't out again until January 1991, when he started working at Newcastle Apartments. He was thirty-eight, with a wife and two sons, one aged ten and the other nearly two. The next twenty months were the last time Laraby would be physically free.

★

WHEN I WAS thirteen and visiting family in Belgium, a friend and I went to a water park. As I waited in my one-piece bathing suit in line for the slide, the older boys behind me began talking about my thighs and ass in French. I tried to ignore them, but then they reached out their hands and stroked down from the small of my back, over my buttocks, and down my thighs to my knees. Stuck halfway up a ladder, I meekly swatted their hands away as they laughed.

When I was fourteen, walking home from the school bus stop one afternoon, a man asking for directions from his car beckoned me closer and closer, saying he couldn't hear me. Stepping forward one cautious foot at a time, I saw that he had his fly open and his penis in his hand, and I froze in terror. I'd never seen a man's erect penis before. He drove off, laughing.

When I was fifteen, my family went out to dinner in Perth Amboy. As we walked along the pier afterward, my sister and I about ten feet behind my parents, a clearly drunk man approached me. "You're so beautiful," he said, and I froze in fear as he caressed my face.

These were still knife-sharp images in my mind when I heard that a guy suspected in Stephanie's disappearance (I didn't then know Laraby's name) had been arrested for assaulting Bethany Swenson, a girl my age.

It would be a few years more before a guy broke into my college dorm room, watched me sleep, and masturbated onto a T-shirt I had folded up on my desk; before my friend was raped by a mutual friend of ours; before another friend told me about how as a child, she was forced to watch her father rape her sister; and even longer before the night, as a woman of thirty-five, when I agreed to have sex with a guy I went on a date with—as long as he wore a condom. But he didn't have a condom, and he said, "You're not going to make me take it from you, are you?" and I froze, the same way I had in the street when I was fourteen, and it happened, anyway, even though I didn't want it, leaving me ashamed.

The things men do to women in this world.

34

THE SAME DAY I first meet Sandra in her office, in June 2015, I have an appointment with Bob Napier, Laraby's last defense lawyer, whom he retained after Stephanie's remains were found and he learned he was a person of interest.

We meet at his office in downtown Rochester, a five-minute walk from Sandra's. Napier is a man of imposing height with a strong hand-shake and thick white hair. I've heard rumors he was a pet lawyer of the Hells Angels.

Napier is the only person involved in the case who declines when I ask if I can record our conversation. Napier is also the only person I meet who seems to have any shred of sympathy for Laraby.

"He had a mirthful, charming side. He was a very likable man whose criminal record said you should be very scared of him," Napier says with a smile, before adding that Laraby admitted that there was something irrevocably wrong with him.

"There was a real sickness," Napier tells me. In 2012, Laraby himself wrote, "I am what psychiatrists call a sociopath. I can assure you for better or worst [sic] that I am not burdened by morality, ethics, or remorse, and I certainly do not posses [sic] a conscience that needs to be cleansed."

Although Bob Napier says Laraby "believed in the immortality of the soul," he adds that Laraby "wanted it very clear that he didn't feel remorse."

I find myself wondering about Laraby's childhood, wanting details. My mission to find anyone who knew Laraby in school fails. I track down alumni from the two high schools he attended—from the classes of 1971, when Laraby would have been eighteen, and 1972. They don't remember him. Only one man responds to me, saying he has a faint memory of Laraby's name and a fuzzy image of a boy wearing "a white T-shirt like the Fonz from Happy Days," a boy who seemed tough and hard to handle, who took shop class and "wasn't that intellectual." But he can't say for certain it was Laraby. "The name rang a bell" is the best he can tell me.

Over a year after our first meeting, I follow up with Bob Napier to ask him what, if anything, he knows about Laraby's childhood. It's a cold, cloudy October morning, and it's a mournful conversation we have. Napier's capacity for empathy for the broken parts of the worst imaginable criminals is beginning to shift in my perspective. He is a fearless man in this regard, and the only one who can tell me much about Laraby as a child.

Laraby made sure to tell him everything, Laraby said, in anticipation that one day someone might want to write about him. "What I was told by Ed is completely anecdotal," Napier tells me on the phone.

He means none of it can really be confirmed—although a lot of it lines up with the story from the intake forms on the CD Sandra gave me, when Laraby tried to check into Park Ridge Hospital in 1992. He may have made up the whole thing. But this is the version Laraby told Napier.

★

LARABY'S MOTHER ALICE gave birth to him on February 20, 1953, in Binghamton, New York. She was in her late teens, and married to his biological father, Donald, at the time, but they divorced while Laraby was an infant.

Soon after the divorce, Alice met Harold Laraby, an older man who adopted baby Ed and gave him his last name. The small family moved to Rochester, and Alice and Harold had three more children.

In 1959, when Ed was six years old, Harold moved the family to Kokomo, Indiana, where his older children lived. Although he'd given Laraby a surname, he didn't take much interest in him. While Harold was the main disciplinarian when it came to his younger kids, he never laid a hand on his stepson Ed. He left that to Alice.

Laraby told Napier his mother hit him with her hands and fists, with electrical cords, with belts and paddles. She'd lock him in a dark, dirt-floored root cellar filled with bugs, mice, and rats for hours at a time. "Fifty years later, he'd totally freak out if a bug landed on him," Napier says.

In 1962, when Ed Laraby was nine years old, his mother died of lung cancer and pneumonia; she was twenty-seven, the same age Stephanie was when she was killed. Alice had never hugged or kissed Ed, as far as he could remember, only beaten him daily.

Ed was fairly alone in Kokomo; his stepfather was busy with his own kids. A local adult took advantage of the situation and began to sexually abuse Ed Laraby.

Laraby didn't mourn his mother. She was buried in Indiana, and Harold moved the family back to Rochester soon after. Harold had frequently told Laraby that he wasn't his father. But when Harold sat him down two months later and said it again, now that his mother was dead, it meant more. It meant, I'm not responsible for you. It meant: you are alone now.

Laraby was dumped in Rochester with his mother's parents, older, dysfunctional alcoholics who seemed to have little interest in raising a ten-year-old. His grandparents passed him to his biological father, and his stepmother, who also beat him.

After six months, he was returned to Alice's parents in Rochester, where he stayed for one week before they drove him back to Binghamton. No one answered the door at his father and stepmother's house, so his grandparents said, "Sit on the porch. They'll be along soon," and left him with a cardboard box containing all his earthly belongings.

Ten-year-old Ed Laraby waited a while, alone, then walked to the neighbor's house. "Oh, they're away on vacation for two weeks," the neighbors said. "We've been picking up their mail."

His grandparents were long gone, so the boy ambled his way to downtown Binghamton.

For two or three weeks he lived a runaway's life with another kid he met downtown, stealing what they needed to survive and sleeping in alleys. Eventually the cops picked him up and deposited him at the Susquehanna Valley Home for Orphans. Laraby stayed in the gray, gabled, looming building, living an Oliver Twist life, for two years. He attended Benjamin Franklin Elementary School nearby, broke curfews and missed bed checks. After four or five transgressions, he took off to find his stepfather up near Rochester. He was thirteen.

This time, Harold let him stay.

★

HAROLD LARABY RAN a scrap-metal yard in Fairport, and Ed was old enough to be of use. Ed described Harold for Napier: "He was never really a bad guy, but we were never close. He had ulterior motives."

All through middle school, Laraby worked at the scrap-metal yard. (This was around the time of the fire that killed sixteen of the family's rabbits.) But eventually he tired of living with his stepfather and of the manual labor, so he moved in with his middle school girlfriend and her older sister. In 1968 he started going to Brighton High School, where, Napier says, "he felt like the odd man out in a very foreign environment of kids from mostly good backgrounds."

His teen romance soon faded, and so did his living situation. Laraby came home from school one day to find another cardboard box full of his possessions unceremoniously dumped on the front porch. The message was clear: "You don't live here anymore."

Then almost sixteen years old, Laraby turned to his stepfather's brother, a police officer, for help. His step-uncle brought him to a social worker who found Laraby a foster home in Webster. He transferred to Webster High School.

His foster parents were nice people. Napier calls them "goody-two-shoes" and says Laraby described the wife as "June Cleaver." Laraby, on the other hand, was getting drunk two or three nights a week and smoking marijuana almost every day. He couldn't connect with his foster parents, and he didn't fit in; it was only a few months before he moved to another foster home and transferred to East High School in Rochester.

Laraby told Napier that his first day of school at East was the first day the school began busing black students from another area in accordance with a controversial desegregation plan. His memories of the school were tied up with memories of racially charged altercations.

Laraby told Napier he went to Woodstock with friends. It was 1969—the year of the car accident that knocked out his teeth, and around when Laraby dropped out of school and returned once more to his stepfather's house in Fairport. It was also around the time he got arrested for driving without a license. He told Napier that he'd gotten boisterous in court, "cracking wise" with the judge, who said, "As a lesson, you'll spend fifteen days in jail. You've got to learn, son."

In 1971 Laraby got an apartment and started working in a bar. He had no real friends, no direction, no high school diploma. Feeling alone and aimless, he thought he'd give military life a whirl.

But it was too late for him to straighten out. He couldn't be saved by anything. He seemed to know this to a degree, too.

★

YEARS LATER, IN 1992, a few weeks after Annette's rape, Laraby would sit across from the intake counselor at Park Ridge and say, "I don't know what love is." He admitted that he often alleviated his rage by taking it out on innocent strangers, "if they took the bait."

"One of these days," Laraby told the counselor, "some sucker is going to catch twenty years of wrath."

★

LARABY'S CHILDHOOD—ALL THAT abandonment, violence, and sexual abuse—sounds to me like a recipe for a sociopath. After hearing what Napier has to say, I feel surer than ever that he was. I have research to do. When I get back to Brooklyn, I buy three books on the topic.

In his book *Murderous Minds*, neurobiologist Dean A. Haycock explains that technically, there is no medical or scientific distinction between the terms *sociopath* and *psychopath*; he prefers to use *psychopath*. His book describes the intricacies of the brain of a psychopath, differentiating between the criminal or unsuccessful psychopath and the successful psychopath who manages to stay above the law.

Laraby is a textbook case: he meets the conditions for a diagnosis of antisocial personality disorder, and even for the label of "conduct disorder" that gets applied to children. In his childhood, he exhibited aggression and destructive tendencies; he stole, ran away from home, and skipped school.

Yearning for a fuller understanding of a mind like Laraby's, I email Dr. Haycock, and then we talk on the phone for an hour. Haycock's voice is gentle and unobtrusive. He doesn't speak so much as an authoritative expert as someone, like me, intently curious.

I emailed Haycock with Laraby's name the day before, and he has pored over what he found online. As he starts to share his insights, I can feel myself grappling with what will become, and remain, a complicated emotional dynamic for me. Whatever else he was, and whatever he might have done, Laraby was a human being, and a product of a devastating upbringing. And yet so many people in this story survived abusive childhoods—including Stephanie and myself. So what sets someone like Laraby apart? What pushes someone from the vitriol and fire of someone like me to the manipulation of someone like Stephanie's ex-boyfriend Geoff? And then what creates the type of amoral, violent serial rapist Laraby was?

In our conversation, Dr. Haycock explains that psychopathy is not so much a clear diagnosis as it is a collection of traits and behaviors. Psychopaths show serious deficits in morality, ethics, guilt, regret, and reflection, all things Laraby lacked and copped to lacking. They don't tend to learn from punishment and can't be rehabilitated, only noting the personal benefits of their actions and not the negative results, which might be why jail wasn't a real deterrent for Laraby.

They can recognize morally objectionable behavior, but it's only as if they've learned by rote what everyone else believes is moral. Often psychopaths have "the gift of gab," sometimes able to deftly convince parole boards to release them; Haycock relates the story of Jack Abbott, a killer who convinced the author Norman Mailer to champion his parole request, then stabbed a man to death six weeks after he was out. Yet psychopaths display a severe disconnect between their words and their emotions; Laraby often laughed while speaking of atrocious things. It's said that psychopaths know the words but not the music.

So Laraby could acknowledge that stealing from the elderly was wrong, and warn people about it in his Seventh Stepper advice column.

He could urge women like Annette to take better precautions, to lock their doors with deadbolts and their windows with bars. But he couldn't stop himself from intruding when they didn't. It was as if he felt it was someone's own fault if they were stupid enough to stay vulnerable.

Laraby told Bob Napier that if someone wrote about him, maybe people could learn to be more aware of these things, that the idea of "stranger danger" could be reinforced. "It wouldn't just be a blood and gore story," Napier said to me, as though spurring me on. "There would be a societal benefit."

Of course, a psychopath like Laraby would be motivated also by the narcissistic impulse to have his name published, his crimes memorialized.

One thing is certain to Dr. Haycock: the brains of psychopaths are markedly different from those of nonpsychopaths. Certain zones—the amygdala and frontal cortex, for example—exhibit drastic abnormalities in brain scans. Haycock says these abnormalities can be caused by a slew of different things: "stroke, head trauma, or genetics combined with a damaging environment. In the case of born or developmental psychopaths, bad luck with regard to genetics and upbringing can impair function in the key brain regions."

Someone can be born with these genetic predispositions but be raised in a loving home, and escape becoming this type of monster. Or, conversely, someone can be beaten and belittled every day of their lives yet not develop the brain dysfunctions that equate with psychopathy.

In other words, it could be a tragic confluence of the trifecta of genetics, brain abnormalities, and a damaging environment—sometimes not even all three. So what creates a person like Laraby, and what prevents someone like me, or Geoff, or Stephanie, from becoming a sociopath might be random, ill-fated coincidence.

After I tell Dr. Haycock the story of Laraby's childhood, he says, in a voice tinged with sorrow, "These people do suffer. They can't get pleasure from the things we do. Nobody should live a life like that."

35

OFFICER PATRICK KEALY was alone in a hospital room with Edward Laraby—who was then seven years into the twenty-five-year sentence Judge Bergin had handed down—on a Sunday morning in July 2001. It had been three years since Stephanie's bones were found, and three years since Jerry cut off contact with Laraby.

Laraby was being monitored in Auburn Memorial Hospital's coronary care unit, having complained of chest pains three days before. The other security officer stepped out for a moment.

Kealy had his back turned, and Laraby saw his chance. He jumped from the bed with monitor wires in his hands, wrapped the wires around Kealy's neck, and pulled so hard Kealy was lifted up from his chair. Kealy struggled. Laraby punched him in the head several times.

Kealy and Laraby struggled as they both reached for Kealy's revolver, but hospital workers heard the commotion and came running. They pulled Laraby away and held him down long enough for Kealy to subdue him. He was brought straight back to jail.

Laraby claimed he didn't intend to kill Kealy; he only wanted to escape because other inmates at Auburn Correctional Facility were threatening him. Indeed, he had been stabbed by another prisoner in retaliation for cooperating with prison officials trying to track down illegal weapons. And although he was placed in protective custody after the stabbing, the threats continued.

He was found guilty of two counts of attempted murder and one count of attempted escape. Two more twenty-five-to-life sentences were handed down, to be served concurrently—beginning after the one he was currently serving for assaulting Bethany Swenson.

For the next eight years he tried appeal after appeal on his own behalf. His last attempt was in 2009. "The Court finds no merit to the defendant's remaining contentions," county judge Thomas Leone wrote.

It was over. Laraby's chances for parole had evaporated. He would never get out. He would never again hide in the bushes and attack another woman on a bicycle, would never again sneak into an apartment to watch a woman sleep, would never again grab a teenager by her crotch as she walked with a friend.

But at the time, in 2009, I didn't know that part of the narrative. Once David Connors retired and my stepfather began declining, the family fell out of touch with the cops, and there was not much news about progress into Stephanie's murder. As far as I knew, he would be up for parole in 2017. I was terrified at the idea of a free Laraby, of the man who likely killed Stephanie being anywhere but behind bars. Imagining him collecting his belongings and walking out into the sunshine, I would shudder.

Then there was also the possibility that Laraby was not the man who had killed Stephanie. There was no real evidence he was, after all, just speculation. Numerous people believed that Laraby was not the man who killed Stephanie. Michael Gately, in Martha's Vineyard, still thought Geoff Fletcher was responsible. And until her death in 2008, Stephanie's own "Baba"—Jerry's mother—held fast to the idea that it was Tom Redmond. Still others thought it might be some serial killer, a Shawcross copycat, John White, or some other man.

If Laraby was the one who'd killed Stephanie and he stayed in jail, we were safe. But if he wasn't, it didn't matter how long he stayed in prison. Her murderer could still be out there. And whoever he was could hurt someone else.

No matter what, with back-to-back sentences at a minimum of twenty-five years each, Laraby would die behind bars, trapped like a rabbit in a burning barn.

36

STAN CHIZUK AND Mike Ives were assigned Stephanie's cold case in 2009 and quickly set their sights, with a striking exclusiveness of focus, on Laraby. In their estimation, he was the most likely suspect in Stephanie's death, and their main goal was to get him to say so.

They started with Terry, Laraby's ex-wife, who asked, "Is that asshole dead yet?" Terry claimed she hadn't spoken to Laraby in years, though he had recently started writing her letters, asking for money for a TV, saying he had cancer. This, if true, was news to Stan and Mike, and might provide them a way in.

They confirmed with Great Meadow Correctional Facility that Laraby had non-Hodgkins lymphoma and liver and kidney cancer. "If you want to talk to him, you better do it soon," they were told.

On October 27, Stan and Mike wrote to Great Meadow and asked to have a meeting with Laraby. "We would request that the inmate Laraby **not be advised** of our pending visit and that this matter be kept confidential," they wrote, planning to catch Laraby off guard. The prison agreed.

When they went to visit him, and he found out that they were cops, Laraby said, "Fuck you. I'm not talking to you." The meeting lasted about a minute.

They needed a way to pique Laraby's interest. They turned to Laraby's prison counselor—"the only guy he talked to, his only outlet," Stan says—who relayed their messages to Laraby. "Tell him we can make his life more comfortable," they said, and to make it clear they wanted to talk about Stephanie.

They left some reports and photos with Laraby's counselor, including Annette's harrowing statement after she was raped.

Later the same day, the counselor called Stan to tell him he'd read Annette Alferov's words to Laraby, who became "visibly upset," said he felt sick, and went back to his cell "to think." "I think he might want to talk in the future," the counselor told Stan.

Wanting to maintain momentum, Stan planned to write to Laraby. But they needed an in. Suddenly Stan remembered a girl named Barb Laraby he'd dated years before. She had to be some cousin, something. The coincidence was his key. Using what he got from Connors and from Laraby's 1992 intake form from Park Ridge Hospital, Stan cobbled together a narrative of Laraby's life just imprecise enough to intrigue Laraby.

He started by apologizing:

> I would like to apologize for coming to talk without first asking you. I was truly disappointed that we were not able to have a conversation. Of all the people I have met with, I think you would be one of the most interesting. In my life, I have come to believe that things don't simply happen by coincidence.

Stan went on to report everything he knew of Laraby's childhood and life, citing Laraby's cousin, Stan's ex-girlfriend Barb. He said he hadn't put the names together until he was assigned Stephanie Kupchynsky's case and realized the stories he'd heard from Barb were about Ed Laraby. "It hit me like a ton of bricks," he wrote.

Stan tells me that he wasn't even sure Barb's last name was spelled the same, that they probably weren't even related. But he knew Laraby wouldn't care that he couldn't remember a cousin Barb; he would be more enticed by the fact that someone he didn't remember had noticed and remembered *him*. Stan was riffing when he said Barb's family had said Laraby's stepfather had been abusive toward him but that his mother was a good person. "They guessed things would have been very different for you had she survived," Stan wrote, and, turning philosophical, he added that people are sometimes given the chance, when they reflect on mortality, to resolve some of their conflicts. He went on:

> What is passed onto us and what we feel with our instincts and spirit make up our life. Mr. Laraby, I have seen evil. I have seen the eyes of a man who raped a child. I have seen the battered head of a six-year-old who lay lifeless . . . I can only guess that you have seen many things in your lifetime. Some things may be unresolved. Do you believe that you are worthy of God's humanity or are you different from faithful?

Stan then offered a few personal tidbits. He told Laraby that he was in the US Navy Reserve, a Mason, and a family man. "I like cigars, and having a cold beer and a game on TV is almost perfect. I know the final chapters of my life are mine to write. I only hope I choose the words well."

He closed by saying that although he knew he had no control over Laraby, he thought Laraby might want to have some say in how he could be represented in a book Dave Connors might write about the case. He said there were about to be new DNA tests done on evidence from Stephanie's apartment; if the forensic evidence spoke for itself, Stan said, Laraby's redemption might no longer be under his own control. He offered to bring Laraby's sons to see him as a gesture of good faith, knowing from the counselor that Laraby was hurt that they weren't visiting.

But Laraby's interest had been aroused before he even got the letter. Just after sending his, Stan received a typewritten letter from Laraby in the mail; their letters had crossed. Laraby was direct with his requests and as cocky as ever. He knew why they had come.

> I heard your message that you could make thing's better for me in prison. There are some thing's you can do to make my existense more tolerable and if you comply I will give you an interview that will satisfy you.

First, deposit $9500.00 dollars in my prison account, with a notarized letter that states the money is a gift and not the proceeds of any crime. I am tired of existing on .45¢ a day.

Second, get me transferred to Attica and get me an even numbered cell in the Honor Block. This is not an arbitrary request as the even numbered cells provide the maximum of privacy.

Third, there is a posted reward offered in one case. I want my son to receive this.

These terms are non-negotiable. Meet them and I will make your dreams come true.

Stan had some ammunition now, but he still needed to be careful not to spook Laraby, whose extraordinary demands showed he still thought of himself as a powerful agent of his own destiny rather than a repeat sex offender who was up the river probably until he died. While he was formulating a reply, Laraby responded to Stan's first letter.

Dear Stan,

You asked if I'm religious. I was baptized a Catholic, but that was as far as it went. Currently I am registered as a Rastafarian. An interesting story goes with that and sometime I'll tell you about it.

Christmas is coming and I find myself thinking of my sons. My youngest boy is in the army and is scheduled to deploy to Afghanistan sometime soon. I rarely hear from him. I have been trying to reach my older boy for over a month and have been unable to connect with him. I don't know if it's bad timing on my part or perhaps he's ignoring my calls.

I find this time of year to be trying at best. I usually go through some suicidal idealogy this time of year. I get a bunch of mental health medication and it helps but the urges are strong. As I think about my life and some of the thing's I've done it overwhelms me. Do the holidays cause you any discomfort?

I understand that this is just business for you because you're looking for a resolution to some cases. I'll be honest with you Stan, if my conditions aren't met you will never have a resolution to those cases. One thing you learn in prison is how to lay back and be patient. I'll wait for as long as it takes and eventually I'll die with my secrets intact.

In this letter, Laraby, despite still being full of threats, perhaps unwittingly gave himself away. He had a vulnerability—and that was his kids. Stan's hunch that he could build on Laraby's yearning for his sons was amplified. When the boys were young, Terry had often brought them to the prison for visits, but over time this happened less frequently. And once the boys were of age, they decided they wanted nothing to do with their father.

I think about those boys, growing up with their father in prison, learning what monstrous things he'd done. Both are married, living lives that from the outside probably look normal. But they know who their father was, and I assume it must haunt them. I don't want to bother them to ask. If I have learned anything from my own father, it's that breaking away and creating your own identity is a struggle, and once you've done it, you don't want to look back.

Stan found Laraby's older son, Mark, then twenty-nine, beginning life as a husband and father. He was friendly, but bitter; he told Stan there wasn't much contact with his father except when he wanted money. He'd even thought about changing his albatross of a surname.

Neither of the sons wanted to see their father again, but Laraby didn't need to know that. Better to tantalize him with the promise of reconciliation.

Stan was cautious, methodical. Nothing anyone had ever tried before had worked. "They all hit him with the here-and-now," Stan says. "I hit him with things he didn't expect."

If Laraby did kill Stephanie, there was no reason for him to confess. His sentences were too long to hope for leniency or a chance at parole. All he did in prison was create drama. He'd registered as a Rastafarian so he could keep his long gray beard, and had registered a complaint with the state in 2006 that he was being harassed and accosted because of his religion. That trial took place just after he started corresponding with Stan; the claim was quickly dismissed.

Laraby wasn't going to cooperate with Stan and Mike unless they made him dependent on them. That's what they intended to do.

Stan got in touch with Steven Conlon at the Behavioral Science Unit of the FBI in Washington, D.C., and picked his brain for tips on manipulating Laraby. Play to his weaknesses. Give him some of what he wants. Keep him wanting more. Pay attention to details. In his tight handwriting, a mishmash of cursive and print, with tiny vowels, Stan took notes: "Minimize victim's importance. Make Ed explain: 'What is your most memorable rape?' Monitor body language compared to words, descriptions, voice inflection. Schedule a meeting with him and cancel. Always bring less than promised. Large pizza = small pizza."

He sent a copy of the entire case file to Conlon in D.C. and plotted his next move.

In the interim, Laraby wrote a third time. Now his letter was handwritten in right-slanting cursive, as if he were a fifth-grader trying hard to write neatly. Once Laraby shifted to writing by hand, his letters took on a more personal, intimate tone.

Written on November 17, 2009—five days before my stepfather would die—this third letter read:

> You paint a decent picture of my mother, in fact she was a terribly evil woman. Yes she died of cancer when I was nine, but the damage she done haunted me throughout my life.
>
> She used to strip me naked and beat me with an electrical cord. One time she beat me with a thorny switch and the thorns tore my flesh open. She punched me in the face more times than I can count. I remember my stepfather holding me over the sink and pulling clots from my nose. So don't give my mother any decent words, she doesn't deserve it.
>
> Yes my biological father was an abusive drunk and I lived with my grandparents for a short time. When my mother died

[an adult] used me sexually for several months. His way of consoling me I guess.

You talk about humanity in your letter. I haven't been human for a very long time. At times I can relate to humanity but more times than not I find it an alien concept.

Whether or not his allegations were true, the letter seemed to be an appeal to Stan's sympathy. Stan could see that, so he wrote back:

I am glad you wrote. Obviously, our first letters crossed in the mail. I am looking into your requests. I will always be honest with you and not lie, no matter how things go. Stephanie's family has changed a great deal since then and they have, over time, distanced themselves from us. That does not keep us from accommodating your requests. For what it's worth, it's respectable that you're trying to take care of Mark. If I can help you with that, I will.

I had no idea how much you endured as a child. Unless you have walked in that person's shoes, you really don't know them. I am not going to insult you with a lot of BS about how bad you had it. I do agree life experience plays a large role in the total sum of a person. As far as not being human, I see the man you are and the man you want to be and someday those two will meet. I thank you for giving me a glimpse into your world. It helps put things in perspective.

It dawned on me after your last letter that it is costing you money to send them. I am going to send some money to your commissary for you to use if you want to write again. Keep in mind that if you would like to visit with Mark, I will bring him out no strings attached.

The bait was set.

37

O NE TUESDAY MORNING in November 2009, the hospice doctors
told my mother Jerry would die that day. I raced to New Jersey
from Brooklyn. Jerry held on for five more days, breathing, fidgeting
uncomfortably, and shifting his eyes around the room, but otherwise
silent.

On the third day, Melanie, my mother, and I were sitting around
Jerry at his deathbed, classical music in the background as always, when
a hot and swirling energy seemed to fill the room. None of us spoke for
a long time while the vibrations intensified, and even the light seemed
to take on a golden hue. I could have sworn that Stephanie was there
with us, on her hands and knees at the foot of the bed, deliriously happy,
as joyful and ebullient as only a ghost could be, waiting for her dad. "Is
that crazy?" I asked my mom and Mel.

"So weird," said Mel. "I felt that my late conductor Georg Solti was
here, whispering in my ear, 'Coraggio!'"

"And Nino was here, just standing quietly behind me," said my mom,
referring to her late first husband, the man to whom she was married
before she met my father.

After that, Jerry kept breathing for two more days, but he was still, his
eyes fixed and unmoving. He died on November 22. He was eighty-one
years old.

★

LARABY'S NEXT LETTER to Stan was written November 29, 2009, the Sunday after Thanksgiving, one week to the day after Jerry's death. The letter was plaintive, almost desperate:

> So Stan, are you trying to be my friend or is it because you want something from me? To tell you the truth, I could use a friend. Being a sex offender in prison is hard because no one wants to know or associate with you. You can keep the secret until someone exposes you and they always expose you. They turn on you like a pack of rabid dogs. Even other sex offenders turn on you because they don't want to be exposed. Subsequently it is a lonely existence. I have no friends or even associates. I walk in the darkness afraid to move in the light. Light always means exposure and hatred. Everyone hates a sex offender, fellow prisoners, guards, and civilians alike. They don't understand that it's a sickness. So if you don't hold it against me being a sex offender, I won't hold it against you that you're a policeman.
>
> You mentioned a book deal. Who is the author? The name Connors comes to mind. He tried to communicate with me but I wasn't feeling his energy. I suppose the book will make me out to be a monster. I suppose I am to normal people.
>
> No one is sorrier than I am for things I've done, but sometimes I'm sorry doesn't mean much. My mother created a monster. Now I'm sitting here with double life wondering why it had to be me.
>
> I don't know if you know but I have cancer. I recently had eight treatments of chemotherapy and it is in remission. So I'm going to die in prison. Not the kind of end I envisioned.

It takes me three readings to understand that Laraby did not mean he was living a "double life," one as a monster and one as a human being, but that he was doing two life sentences. I ask Stan about this letter—about Laraby saying he was sorry. "Remorse is different than regret," Stan says. "He regretted he got caught, that he couldn't continue his behavior and the things he did. He had some type of normalcy—maybe with his kids, maybe around the holidays. There was something that would be normal to him. That's not the same as remorse."

Stan says Laraby tried to kill himself a few times, too—that while they were in touch, he began to hoard pain meds and planned to take them all. "Or maybe he was going to trade with other inmates for other stuff. It's hard to say what his real motives were."

Regardless, Laraby was hooked on Stan's letters. He longed for human connection, even from a police officer. Stan replied, trying to give Laraby what he craved. He'd called himself a monster, so Stan assured him he wasn't, especially if he was drunk or high when he did the terrible things he did. He said Laraby was more than the sum of his actions. "You can not change your past," Stan wrote, "but why let your past define your future?"

"I have known quite a few sex offenders, both professionally and personally, and I agree it is a sickness," he went on. He confided that he himself hadn't spoken with his father in six years, that he understood the ways family trauma can work its way into a person's entire existence, affecting them forever. And he talked again about religion, saying he was something of a disloyal Catholic and that, as we were all responsible for our own spirituality, he wished Laraby would free himself from worrying about what others thought of him.

He closed by offering to visit Laraby for the holidays, to talk and get to know one another.

But Laraby wanted to test him first. On December 17, as my mother prepared for her Christmas without her "Ukie"—as she called Jerry—Laraby replied, twisting Stan's words.

> You asked if there was anything you could do for me for the holidays. There are a couple of things. I need a pair of sneakers size 11.
>
> Also, I'm allowed to have a food package sent from home in two 20 lb. packages. It's the facility rule. If you could get some beef jerky and an assortment of cookies and candy and send two 20 lb. packages to me. If you can't do it, no big deal. I'll live, sorry to say.

You were asking about a face-to-face meeting. I'm going to think about that for a while.

You said you thought I was an interesting person. In actuality, I'm quite boring. I spend about 95 percent of the time in my cell. (By choice.) I suffer from apathy. It's hard to get out of bed in the morning. Some days I long for people, but people can't stand the sight of me. Basically I'm tolerated because I'm old and harmless. Believe me 56 is old compared to the average prisoner. We've got 17-year-olds here. They should be looking for prom dates not wasting away in a cage.

His requests were as specific as a child's Christmas wishlist. He folded his letter inside a Christmas card with Santa on the front, his sleigh sporting two American flags. Inside, he wrote, "Seasons greetings to you and your family."

Stan and Mike went to the supermarket and threw together a box of snacks for Laraby. Stan wrote another letter and put it in the box, too. He urged Laraby to talk to the young guys in prison and help straighten them out. Then he pushed the idea that theirs was a fateful interaction. "I still say things don't happen by chance. You and I were meant to cross paths for a reason." And he planted the idea of a visit. "I may have to go up to Massena sometime and would love to stop in."

Stan had no plans to go to Massena.

He promised he was looking into Laraby's demands, waiting for clearance on the sneakers, although there was some pushback on the $9,500 he wanted—of course that wasn't happening, but Stan made it sound possible. Before the package reached Laraby, Stan got another letter, written January 7, 2010.

In this letter, Laraby explained he wanted the money for a proper burial. "I don't want to be a burden on my family or the state," he claimed. "I also don't want to end up in a pauper's graveyard."

He pondered his mortality more and more. He remained despondent about his sons' detachment, too. Recently, he'd called Mark, but Mark hung up on him. "I don't know what's going on," he wrote. Laraby seemed oblivious as to why his sons might not want contact with him.

"For some unknown reason he is turning his back on me. Maybe you could call him and find out what's wrong."

When the food package with cookies and candy arrived, Laraby wrote again. "They had a fit about the letter, but gave it to me anyways, I appreciate what you did and to be truthful I wasn't expecting it to happen."

Laraby subsequently asked again for a pair of sneakers—"size 11 with good arch support." And if Stan was going to be in the area, Laraby said, "I guess it would be ok if you stopped by. It has to be neutral conversation. I don't know what we'll talk about, but I know what we won't be talking about."

So, he knew what Stan and Mike were after. And if he did indeed have what they wanted—a confession to killing Stephanie—he wasn't going to give it to them easily.

In another letter written on January 18, Laraby asked for a belt, too, and gave more details about the sneakers he wanted—they couldn't have blue or the word "Air" on them, according to prison rules. "If you go with basic black, you can't go wrong, but use your judgment."

Even though Laraby still seemed reticent to talk about Stephanie, his eagerness for Stan's visit was growing obvious, acute, childlike even. He wrote, "Do you have a date that you were planning on coming up? If I know when you're coming, I won't stray far from my cell so I'll be available. I don't want to make you wait while they locate me. I haven't had a visitor in quite a while, like 6 or 7 years."

Something good had already come from the letters—possible DNA evidence. Stan's partner Mike Ives sent Laraby's envelopes and the twenty-year-old evidence from Stephanie's apartment—the mattress cover with the small stain, the floral shorts, white tank top, and Keds—to the lab to search for a DNA match.

There wasn't one.

38

O N JANUARY 19, 2010, with no real evidence to leverage, Stan and Mike drove over 250 miles to Great Meadow Correctional Facility in Comstock, an hour north of Albany, and were brought to a small room where they waited for Laraby to be ushered in.

Laraby had been made out to them to be terrifying, but the man before them wasn't intimidating at all. Rather, he seemed to be barely disguising his vulnerability and desperation for any kind of social contact.

Laraby told them he was a sick man who did bad things because he couldn't control his urges and thought about sex all day, every day. "My head would be on fire with the thoughts," Laraby said. But the chemo had extinguished the thoughts and left him with erectile dysfunction.

He talked about his wife, Terry. He said they were once like Bonnie and Clyde. He said he'd never been caught for robbing the "Spur Bar" in Rochester, a place on Dewey Avenue that is now the Overtime Grill. In fact, the police have no evidence that Terry was involved in any crime or had any inkling about his sexual assaults save the ones for which he'd already been convicted.

Mike told him the statute of limitation was over on the rapes, but they'd sure like to clear them up, especially the assault of Annette Alferov. "Newcastle Complex should be sued for ever giving me keys," Laraby said. Stan and Mike looked at each other. Both were thinking, "This is our guy."

Laraby said he'd talk if Stan and Mike brought a letter from the DA saying he wouldn't be charged. They said they'd try, and promised to work on the sneakers and belt.

"Is there anything you want us to bring when we come back, Ed?" Stan asked.

"Yeah," Laraby said. "A Meat Lover's Pizza from Pizza Hut. I haven't had one of those in over twenty years."

Before they left, they told him Stephanie's family had changed a lot in the seventeen years she'd been dead.

Laraby corrected them: "It'll be nineteen."

★

THREE DAYS LATER, Laraby wrote Stan again: "I've been having reservations about the Annette thing. I keep thinking there's another motive other than clearing a case. I keep thinking it will come back and bite me on the ass. What's the rush? I could bare my soul all at once if the conditions are met."

Laraby seemed suspicious, but not ready to walk away. They couldn't risk scaring him off. So, dressed in nonthreatening jeans and sweatshirts, they drove back to Comstock as soon as they had the letter from Sandra Doorley, who was then ADA, stating that Laraby would not be charged for the assault of Annette Alferov. It was January 26, only one week after their first meeting.

They brought a Pizza Hut Meat Lover's Pizza—a small, of course—and set it down in front of him as they took out their tape recorder.

The pizza, in Stan's words, "was a big deal." It proved they were willing to do what Laraby asked. The taste of the chewy dough, the cheap mozzarella cheese, and the overload of pepperoni, ham, sausage, bacon, pork, and beef seemed to trigger a flood of memories in Laraby's mind. Once he started talking, nothing held him back.

Six years later, I listen to the recording of this meeting that Stan has sent me in the mail.

Laraby starts with his abusive mother. "I would have killed her if she didn't die on her own."

As he grew up, he became more antisocial, developing a hateful disdain for women. "One day I just snapped. I wanted to punish women to ease my own pain." I can hear him eating the pizza, his mouth full of meat. "My mother wore glasses, so I picked women that wore glasses and looked like her."

He tells Stan and Mike that in the late 1980s and early 1990s, he committed more than thirty rapes he still remembers in detail.

"Did you ever feel you conveyed your message of hate and anger? Did anything ever happen that let you know your message was clear?" Mike asks him.

"No," he says. "I just used and abused them and tossed them aside."

Stan and Mike work to keep the mood light, even as their stomachs turn. Laraby laughs at his thoughts sporadically, a fast, breathy "Heh, heh" sometimes or, if he thinks the guys are in on the joke, a more hearty, full-voiced "Ho, ho, ho."

"I had two types of victims," he says. "One was a victim of opportunity that I would put no thought or effort into. I always had my knife, rope or duct tape, and something to cover my face."

These were the rapes and assaults like the ones on the Erie Canal towpath years before.

"The second was a victim I would identify and watch for days, sometimes weeks. I'd plan it all out and even fantasize about my intentions beforehand."

Laraby says he mostly wore a hockey mask and broke into women's apartments by prying open their windows. He would threaten them with his knife, tie them up, and force them to have oral, anal, or vaginal sex, then make them take showers after he raped them. "I liked to strip away their self-respect. It made me feel good," he says. "I'd make them say, 'I am a whore' or 'I am a slut.'"

Stan and Mike stay quiet.

He took souvenirs from his victims, usually their underwear, and kept them in a footlocker at home. From time to time, he'd take things out and masturbate while remembering the rape. "It wasn't about sex," he says. "I wanted control and power."

Stan and Mike remain as silent as stone.

As though he's said too much, Laraby suddenly becomes upset, agitated. "Can we stop?" he asks. "Can you come back tomorrow?"

Stan and Mike don't want to stop now that they've got Laraby talking, and they don't know why Laraby does. They've only been in the room a little over an hour, but Mike stops the recording here. They are losing him, they fear. But they agree to stay the night at a nearby motel, and Mike asks, "What can we bring you?"

Laraby wants Egg McMuffins.

★

THE RECORDING STARTS up again the next morning, when Stan and Mike have returned with the Egg McMuffins, after waiting in the car long enough for them to get cold.

"I didn't think you guys were coming," Laraby says. "Sorry I had to bail on you last night. It's the morphine I take for the pain. It's as bad as heroin. You get a jones for it."

I can hear Laraby unwrapping his breakfast and he laughs and says, "Up in the rotunda, some cop I don't know, a big fat guy, he says, 'This rat bastard's going down to have more pizza.'"

Laraby struggles to open his soda can, so Mike offers to help. "Yeah, you get a little grease on your hands and that thing's never coming off," Mike says, making nice.

They've brought the sneakers—cheap and white, not name-brand and black—and the belt—shoddy and vinyl. But they tell Laraby the prison captain is logging them into property.

They talk about his son Mark. Laraby gives them a letter and points to the words "Return to sender." "That's Mark's handwriting," Laraby says.

Stan says he shot the breeze on the phone with Mark for an hour the week before. They tell Laraby he just needs a little time.

"The big thing," Stan goes on, "is helping Mark understand your situation. It's not what he thinks—it's complicated, with the urges. It's not like you had control over any of that. People don't understand that; they think you could've stopped anytime. I've really worked to try to get him to understand that's not the case. You didn't want to do those things. A lot of it had to do with your childhood, the lack of resources. Had you grown up now, probably you wouldn't have been exposed to half the stuff that you were, and things would've turned out differently."

"In them days," Laraby says with an air of relief, "there was no child protective services."

"I think we have a healthy perspective on what you might've been going through," Mike says. "We'll never understand completely what you went through, but we try to respect it. If somebody had come up to you and said, 'You have cancer, and well, that's not good for you. Get rid of that cancer,' you'd laugh at them. 'I can't get rid of cancer; I can't wish that away!' It's the same thing with the other issue; you can't wish it away. You would've wished it away a long time ago."

Mike goes on: "When we speak to you, speaking about this illness is like speaking about your cancer. I don't think that society realizes this is not something you can put into check by snapping your fingers. We were talking last night—you're an easy guy to talk to, you're a nice guy. In a different time, we might've probably sat down at a bar and had a few beers together."

I feel so sad when I hear Mike say this.

After a quiet moment, Stan and Mike explain again that Laraby's confessions of sexual assault will not be used to prosecute him. They just need some horsepower with Sandra Doorley. If they can bring her the facts, close the old rape cases, prove Laraby is for real, they can see about the other things he wants. "We're not gonna leave you high and dry," Stan assures him.

They ask Laraby to recount in detail what they call "the Canal Rapes." He tells them about the mask he wore the summer of '83—a wrinkled face with a pointed chin and fuzzy gray hair. He says one teenager escaped by jumping into the canal and swimming away and another ran across a footbridge into a neighborhood and started banging on a random front door when she realized he was following her. He says one of the girls he assaulted was black; he remembers the mother and daughter whose car he stole; he remembers one woman who was older and had gray hair. "She was complaining that I was assaulting her because she was old," he says, and he laughs.

He tied her hands behind her with "the plastic kind" of handcuffs— "you pull and it goes ch-ch-ch-ch"—and raped her.

"Did you take anything from her?" asks Stan.

"Ha, just her dignity." Laraby laughs again.

He tells them he "did a few prostitutes" in the fall of '83. Flashing a fireman's badge to make them think he was a cop, he picked them up near Lake and Lyell, where Rochester serial killers Shawcross, Spahalski, and possibly White all found victims. Laraby drove them to remote places and raped them, not bothering to cover his face because he "didn't think they were gonna complain."

"You gotta remember there's times I was inactive because I was in prison," Laraby says. Chronologically, they are up to the 1990s.

Once he was out on parole, he says, he went back to raping sex workers. He'd pick them up and take them to Cobb's Hill Park in Rochester, tie them up, assault them, and leave them there, still bound. But mostly, he focused on the women at Newcastle Apartments.

"The nineties I was working at the complex, and it was like a carnival," he says wistfully. "They gave me keys."

"You were a kid in a candy store," Mike says. "I can't believe they did that. It's unbelievable."

"I would say half the maintenance workers were criminals," Laraby says. Again, he offers no proof.

"You know what, though? We're working in Greece, and . . ."

"Half the people are criminals," Stan interjects.

"I'm not sure if it's different anywhere," Mike says.

"People are people," Laraby says.

"Do you remember Annette Alferov?" asks Stan.

"Yeah," Laraby answers.

"Is that one of the ones?" asks Stan.

"Yeah," Laraby answers.

Mike starts shuffling papers, looking for photos of Annette, and Stan says, "I've seen photos. She had glasses, right? Is that how you . . ."

"Mm-hmm," says Laraby.

He tells them he used a crowbar to get in, wore a hockey mask, brought a whiskey and ginger ale she wouldn't drink, and handcuffed and raped her, then laundered her sheets and made her shower. It is exactly what Annette said twenty years before. In the background of the recording, a prisoner or guard whistles an upbeat tune.

"I probably know the answer to this," Mike says, "but why did you have her shower?"

"To get rid of evidence," Laraby says.

"It worked," Mike says.

Laraby laughs.

"You were very smart, the way you did things. I mean, really, you're a very intelligent person," Mike says before he brings out photos and reports from the rapes that happened in other complexes around the same time, the reason for the surveillance detail back in 1992, one just three miles from Laraby's house—a woman in her forties raped by a man in a hockey mask the same night as Annette Alferov.

Laraby says he had nothing to do with it.

"It's so similar, it's almost unbelievable that it wasn't you! If you'd like to change your mind, we'll accept the change at any time."

Laraby keeps laughing but says, "The stuff I was doing was mostly at the complex."

He tells them about "an Asian female" he stalked after he went by her window one night and "the shade was yea high and she was reading, topless."

He used his key to enter her apartment when she wasn't home and called 511 from her phone to get the number, then would call and harass her on the phone, tell her he was watching her. "I found that you didn't have to do anything really in order to get gratification. You could, like, make threats and say things on the phone and get almost the same result." But, he tells Mike and Stan, it was "a matter of time" before he would have assaulted her.

The night Laraby raped Annette, his target was a woman named Christine, who lived in Newcastle, too. But when he knocked on her door, her boyfriend answered, and Laraby scrammed and ran off to Annette's place, narrowly sparing Christine.

"Any other assaults you can remember from the complex?" Mike asks.

"I can't really say," Laraby says.

Beginning to wrap up the conversation after almost two hours, Stan brings the conversation to the topic of assistant district attorney Sandra

Doorley. "We definitely know what you're looking for. That would be done in what they call a proffer or a contract type deal. We really need to know potentially how many homicides there might be. That's important for us to go back to Sandra and say because it gets us horse-power; it gets her attention. They'll know what they're dealing with."

There's a noise in the background—a guard passing by looks through the door. Laraby suddenly goes on high alert, and when Mike offers to wait before continuing, he does. Stan fills the silence.

"This stuff is twenty years old. Some of the goofs that handled this stuff and took notes . . . tips were coming in all the time. I have no clue where half this information came from, but all I need is a number, so I can go back to her and say, 'Hey, there's one, there's two, there's three, there's one to five,' as generically as you make it."

"I can't think of any, um, more," Ed says.

Mike's voice cracks as he says, "We'll speak to Sandra and say Ed tells us we're dealing with one."

Laraby's silence seems a tacit affirmation. This is the moment. They just have to keep him from balking. They need to make some promis-es—try to get Laraby to believe there's a chance at that $9,500 and transfer to Attica he'd asked for.

They are so very close. Stephanie must be "the one" Laraby doesn't deny. They feel so sure of it.

"The wheels move slow, and we're going through people who make decisions above our heads, but honestly, you don't have two better advo-cates than Stan and me," Mike promises.

"Sandra's a good person," Stan says. "She doesn't play any games, and she's been very cooperative with us. We're gonna do whatever we can."

Mike says it's illegal for the DA's office to transfer money to Laraby, so they'll have to be "creative." He also says the easiest way for Laraby to be transferred out would be to offer details on the homicide, since then he would be moved to Monroe County Jail until his trial. "That's where the movement becomes, ironically, easier," he says. "You'd be closer to Mark and Josh. The reality is you'll probably end your life in prison, so we'd like to have you find more quality of life. If that means that we talk about"—Mike pauses, looking for the right words—"that subject matter, we understand what you're asking for. We're not trying to slip one by you. You're not stupid."

Stan jumps in. "Hey, you've been shit on for a long time, and at some point you deserve a break. You're really a kind of a victim in this; you were created by your environment and a lack of resources. There's still some accountability for things that have gone on, but there's a lot of understanding. If you wanna feel more comfortable and closer to your kids or go to Clinton . . ."

"Let's do this," Mike says. "You've helped us. Stan and I believe that when someone helps you, you help them back. We'll put our heads together. We'll make this work."

Laraby is quiet now. Stan and Mike seem nervous they've gone too far, and they start to joke instead.

Stan says, "Absolutely. I mean we got that pizza in here yesterday. We can do about anything! That was the hardest thing we've ever done!"

"Yeah," Laraby says, and laughs.

"I mean, Mike will probably go to jail for bringing contraband in here, but that's all right," Stan says, laughing, too.

"I'm probably gonna get sentenced for these Egg McMuffins, Ed. I hope you appreciate that," Mike riffs.

They all laugh again.

The question seems to hang in the air: Will Laraby really confess? Does he even have anything to confess?

"You OK?" Mike says. "You have any questions for us?"

"No," Laraby says.

They talk about Laraby's upcoming doctor's appointment, to check on the status of his cancer.

"Kind of a heavy question," Mike says, "but are you nervous about dying at all?"

"I know it's coming," Laraby says, laughing again.

"Does that scare you?" Mike asks.

"A little bit," Laraby says. "I'm tired of living, but I'm scared of dying."

"I gotta ask this 'cause I'm just curious," Mike says. "Do you feel any better that you talked about this a little bit?"

"No," Laraby says, and laughs again. "No, I don't feel better."

"There's no weight lifted off you or anything like that? In other words, if you kept these things a secret, when you talked about them, did that cause you to feel a little bit better that you didn't hafta keep them a secret anymore?"

"No," Laraby says, this time more deliberately. "Just . . . No."

39

I T DID NOT cross Stan and Mike's minds to consider any other conclusion to Stephanie's case. They focused on Laraby with sharklike single-mindedness. They kept circling.

Soon after the meeting with Laraby, Stan wrote in his notes, "Build upon Ed feeling scared in prison. Keep reminding him that he is in a dangerous environment. Maintain Ed's dignity: 'Give you the dignity you deserve.'"

When they got back to Greece, Stan had a letter waiting from a frustrated Laraby:

> I finally got the shoes. The captain sat on them for eight days. The belt fits good. The shoes are a different story. You said you were getting me black Nikes, how did I end up with white generics? I don't want to sound ungrateful and I don't want to be a complainer, but there's no arch support. I'd like you to consider getting a pair with good arch support. Such as Nike, Reebok, Fila, and New Balance. I'm not making any demands but I would appreciate it.
>
> Here's something else to consider. If you come up again, consider bringing me a roast beef sub for lunch. Beef is something I never get.
>
> Well, in a couple weeks, I will be 57. Seems ancient to me since I thought I'd be dead by 30. Haha! I feel much older,

must be the chemo. I was thinking about Dave Connors. What if you gave Connors the money and had him give it to me? It's a technicality, but that's what it's going to take, right? He wrote me before and I referred his letter to my attorney Robert Napier. Speaking of him, he'd have a shit fit if he knew I was talking to you. I hate attorneys, they'll double cross you in a heartbeat.

I hope this finds you well.

The level of Laraby's entitlement was staggering, down to listing what sneaker brands were acceptable. He enclosed a letter he'd sent to Mark that was returned and asked Stan to forward it along. The letter to his son, which was typed, read:

Hello Son! I tried to call you and the operator said you put a block on your phone. I don't understand, Mark. What have I done to make you turn your back on me? I have racked my brain trying to figure out what I did and I came up with zero. Is Cindy giving you a hard time about you calling me? Tell me something. It only costs 44 cents to send me an explanation.

I hope this finds you well and Cindy too. I don't know what else to say. Please give me ten minutes of your time and tell me what the problem is. I love you rather you turn your back on me or not, that's not going to change. I need you in my life just as I need Josh.

And then, in his loopy cursive, Laraby wrote, "I love and miss you. Love always, Dad."

It's hard to tell if Laraby felt authentically wronged and sincerely couldn't understand his son's near disowning, or if he was feigning this righteousness.

Stan faxed it all straight to Steve Conlon, and waited to hear his advice on how to proceed. On March 2, he wrote a quick letter back to

Laraby saying he hadn't had much time to talk to the DA, since he'd been busy with the navy in D.C. But he would bring Laraby lunch soon.

★

ON MARCH 9, 2010, first responders arrived at a house in Greece to find three Jamaican men shot and killed.

The triple homicide was national news and consumed the energies of the Greece police—newly under the leadership of Todd Baxter—as well as state and federal authorities. Stan and Mike traveled to Columbus, Ohio, following the trail of the alleged killers, three Jamaican men living illegally in the States and heavily involved in the marijuana trade.

Stan wrote to Laraby in late March 2010, after two weeks in Columbus with Mike, to reassure him they hadn't forgotten about him but had their hands full with the triple killing. Stan informed Laraby that he would be away on a navy job until the end of April, but wanted to come visit soon, and that he was "doing work behind the scenes" for him.

The three homicides proved a perfect stalling tactic. Laraby was now in remission, and they could let him steep a little longer.

At the beginning of July, Stan wrote again. "Mike and I have been gone off and on for the last five months on our three dead Jamaicans," he said. "We are planning to come up around July 21–23, and we'll bring your sub and sneakers. We look forward to shooting the breeze with you; we have some good stories! I can't believe how fast the first half of the year has gone by—I only have twelve months to go to retire. I can't wait!!!"

There. The seed was planted. Stan would retire, and they wanted Laraby to feel he would miss his chance if he didn't move fast. Laraby wrote back. He complained about the summer heat, and asked for the addresses of three old friends, plus some T-shirts—"I need 4XL because I'm fat. I can't have blue, black, grey, or orange. Those are forbidden colors."

Then he wrote, "I was thinking that three dead Jamaicans is a good start. Haha! There are a lot of them in DOCCS [the New York State Department of Corrections and Community Supervision]. As a rule their a dirty breed with bad hygiene skills. I suppose you know what I mean."

("The irony!" Stan remarked to me about this once. "He said he was a Rastafarian!")

Off to Conlon the letter was faxed. They didn't bring a roast beef sub. They needed something from Laraby first—a promise.

When they next met, they kept it light, and they told Laraby they were looking into a cemetery plot for him in Parma, New York, and trying to find a funeral home that would deal with his burial. He was playing them, too, they knew. He still hadn't mentioned Stephanie.

They kept circling. They had one goal and one goal only—get this guy to confess. To even take the time to worry about what would happen if he didn't, or to wonder if their sights were set too narrowly, would cost energy they didn't wish to spare.

Stan left for D.C., and would be gone for the month of September, so Mike took over as pen pal. Laraby asked Mike to get in touch with his doctor, who was "being an idiot," and "rattle his cage" to see what was causing him pain. He asked again for a letter from the funeral home outlining his burial plans, and he told Mike he wanted to lie in state rather than be cremated for two reasons. One, having his ashes scattered would require the help of his sons, but, Laraby wrote, "Since I'm not in good graces, I guess that idea is out the window." Second, Laraby explained, he "had a dream where in the future, man cannot conceive and they populate the earth with reanimated corpses. Silly, right? I'll leave it up to God."

Laraby, raised quasi-Catholic, was beginning to think about the possibility of an afterlife. He did not want his body rotting on prison grounds. He envisioned a green, lush cemetery with trees and sky and a proper headstone with his birth and death dates, unlike the creek where Stephanie lay for seven years, her body torn apart by animals and elements.

Stan was back in October. He sent some T-shirts, which Laraby likely no longer needed now that summer was over. His next letter, while still chummy, turned up the heat:

> Back from DC. I sent more shirts. Mike wanted to send you
> Captain America underwear, but I stopped him, so you owe
> me. Mike and I have a meeting with the funeral director this

week. I am looking to retire no later than September 1, 2011, so we are running out of time. On top of that, our boss is becoming less supportive of us trying to work things out with you. Let us know where you want to be moved for sure so we can start working on that when you decide it is time. You have to make things work for you now. The moon and stars are lined up and we may not be able to be at this spot again.

Truthfully, they weren't out of time—yet. And Baxter was not becoming less supportive. On the contrary, he kept telling them, "Whatever you guys need."

"Every thirty days, they were going up north with Snicker bars," Baxter recalls. "I was waiting for the local newspaper to ask, 'Why are you buying jellybeans?'"

Laraby wrote back to say he only got to keep one white T-shirt because the two black ones were confiscated. "I told you blue, black, grey, and orange are forbidden colors. You must have forgot."

Stan had not forgotten.

Laraby also wanted a 2011 calendar and another belt; the lining fell off the one Stan and Mike gave him nine months earlier, and the vinyl was cracking. "If you can get me a leather belt, they last forever," he wrote.

He was waiting for a decision on yet another appeal. This time, he was appealing his conviction on the attack of corrections officer Patrick Kealy in 2001, claiming prosecutorial misconduct and ineffective assistance of counsel. He was also trying on his own to get transferred to Attica and wanted to hear about that before he started negotiating with Stan and Mike. "I know you're in a hurry to resolve your case, but my hands are tied with proverbial red tape," Laraby wrote, moving his pawns.

Stan wrote, placating, "We don't want to make you feel we're in a hurry. It's been nineteen years and there's very little interest in it. Our only concern is losing the few people we have interested. You deserve to be treated well and we don't want to see you lose out."

On November 10, 2010, the Vay-Schleich & Meeson Funeral and Cremation Chapels in Rochester gave Stan and Mike a letter to pass along to Laraby. It said they agreed to care for him upon his death and bury him in the Oatka Cemetery in Scottsville—"a beautiful and historic cemetery with mature trees situated on well-maintained grounds."

Stan wrote Laraby the next day. They could visit soon, but they needed a reason. "Our efforts in this case are drying up," he lied. "If you (hint) write us and tell us you have stuff to tell us, we might be able to convince our boss for us to come up."

Laraby wrote back, but disclosed nothing relevant. Instead, he talked about his holiday blues and a guy from Rochester who was new at Great Meadow—Robert Spahalski, the serial killer who walked into the Rochester Public Safety building in 2005 to confess to killing four people. Stan wrote back to say he and Mike were sending a package of treats for Christmas, and added some personal experience about the holidays being hard for him, too. "I believe people have the ability to recognize right and wrong and to atone for their actions. It can be frustrating waiting for that person to come to that place in their mind to make things right," Stan wrote. "You still hanging out with the guy from Rochester? I hear he is on the creepy side."

Laraby wrote back after he got the box of cookies and candy. He seemed grateful. "It was kind of you to think about me during the holidays when you're busy with your own lives. I've been feeling suicidal lately. No word from my sons. It's been a year or more since I heard from them."

The only people to whom he had any connection were two police officers trying to get him to say he killed a woman, and a serial killer. "And yes," Laraby wrote, "he is a creepy dude. That's what four homicides will do to you."

He said he was glad to hear they'd settled things with the funeral home, but wanted to be sure he'd have a headstone and cemetery plot. "It's something that has been on my mind," he wrote. He said a CO was complaining that Stan and Mike's letters weren't on letterhead. The same guard was messing with Laraby about his deal: "He said how do you know their not jerking your chain and just saying your burial arrangement's are in order? It's a fair question. Can you respond to that? I'd like to think everything's above the board's, that's why I wanted something in writing."

Stan let almost a month go by while he and Mike worked on the triple homicide. Then he wrote—on letterhead this time:

> As far as the CO, most of them are worse than the people they are guarding. I would say you are an intelligent guy who has been around the block and can tell when someone is full of shit. I told you I would never lie or mislead you. The burial is real and in writing. It was not easy to put together some of the details. We will give you the necessary documents and go over them when we see you. We have nothing to gain by jerking you around. Obviously we would like to resolve Stephanie's case because it is the right thing to do and truthfully I have an interest in what happened to Stephanie in her last moments of life. I am not sure why it is important to me to know; I did not know her or her family. But like I told you way back, there was a reason we were all drawn together. I do not think it was by accident.

Laraby wrote back, evading Stan's suggestions. He mentioned that his doctor wanted him to undergo "exploratory surgery" to see why he was still suffering even with his cancer in remission; he was having painful muscle cramps and spasms they couldn't explain. "I told him I'm not interested in getting cut open, but he's going to blackmail me into it or cut off my meds."

Stan was out of patience. None of this meant Laraby had definitely killed Stephanie, or if he had, that they could prove it.

40

THAT SPRING, STAN got word from the Navy Reserve that the Joint Task Force Guantanamo at the Naval Base Guantanamo Bay in Cuba needed him. He would be one of a handful of lieutenants to work there from 2011 to 2012.

Stan was set to head to Cuba right after his retirement in April 2011. He was out of time to convince Laraby to confess.

He sent a final letter:

> As things go in life, we can not predict how things will turn out. I have been activated with the Navy to go to Cuba and watch prisoners for a year. I will be leaving at the end of April and will not come back to the police department. I am glad to have met you and developed a relationship with you. It is all part of the rich tapestry of life. I have no idea how this case will be handled when I leave and it looks like Mike will be reassigned and will not have it. I started this with you and would like to see things resolved for you. If you want to make things happen, let me know ASAP. I have until the middle of April and then that is it, my friend. If you want me to come up, have a CO call me so we are not losing time with the mail. If not, I understand the time was not right and with that, I would wish you well and peace in your life.

The phone rang soon. Not wanting to lose all opportunity to get what he wanted, Laraby was ready to talk about Stephanie—in exchange for the promise of a private burial upon his death. And so, on April 5, 2011, Stan and Mike made the drive again.

This time, they brought Laraby the roast beef sub he kept asking for. They watched him eat it, mayonnaise dripping into his beard as he laughed through his confession. Stan says it's a sight he'll never forget.

Laraby told them that on July 31, 1991, he walked to Stephanie's house to say hello. He rang the doorbell, and she answered the door and invited him in. They sat on her couch and started talking. She even played the violin for him a little. Stan and Mike listened but felt unmoved. They couldn't imagine that Laraby would have been welcome in Stephanie's apartment. They wondered what Laraby was leaving out.

But as long as he said one simple thing—that he had killed Stephanie— they would be able to charge him. They were curious, but in the end, it didn't matter that he wasn't telling the whole story—and they were sure he wasn't. They felt sure he was guilty, and if he gave them just enough to believe, they would give him what he wanted. Just like his admitting to the rape of Annette Alferov, this wasn't some attempt to come clean and find absolution; this was a means to an end.

Laraby said that he and Stephanie had been chatting for two hours when she finally reached out to touch him. He put his arm around her to make a move. But he must have misinterpreted her touch, and she screamed. To quiet her, he tightened his arm around her neck and kept it there. When she suddenly began to choke and vomit he let go, and found she wasn't breathing.

"I pulled her onto the floor and did CPR for about a half hour," Laraby said. "I cried for about an hour, and then I cleaned up the apartment."

Stan and Mike cast dubious looks at one another. They found it diffi- cult to believe that a person as dark-hearted as Laraby would have shed tears over Stephanie's death.

Laraby said once he realized Stephanie could not be resuscitated, and wept over that, he wiped his prints off everything and vacuumed, then wrapped Stephanie's body in the sheets from her bed and put her in the trunk of her car.

Then he drove out to Orleans County. He took Stephanie's body from the trunk, walked into a field, and removed her clothes "so she would decompose faster."

He got back in the car to drive back to Greece, throwing her checkbook out the window along the way. "I hoped that the checkbook being found by someone else would throw the police off my track and the finder of the checkbook would be a suspect," he said. It was exactly what happened to Chris Mosher.

He parked her car at the airport so people would think she traveled somewhere, threw her car keys into the canal, and took a cab home.

And, just like that, it all seemed to be over. Ed Laraby had confessed to the murder of my stepsister, Stephanie Kupchynsky. Stan finished transcribing the narrative he'd handwritten (Laraby's motor functions were by then so diminished that he could barely hold a pen) and put it in front of Laraby, who scrawled his initials at the bottom of the confession.

It was all so matter-of-fact. The end of a twenty-year journey, an indisputably brilliant combination of cunning and patience—arguably the pinnacle of their careers as police detectives. So why did it feel like such an anticlimax? Laraby had confessed to a homicide; they could charge him, and that was good.

Still, it didn't sit quite right with Stan and Mike. Everything Laraby told them was public knowledge; nothing was information only her killer would have known. It was the kind of confession anyone could have put together if they'd researched the case at all. It just didn't feel *done*. They wondered again what Laraby was leaving out.

And why bullshit them? They kicked it around together and had three possible answers.

One, he wanted to keep as clean an image as possible for his sons' sake. He knew they'd suffered for his name, and he felt guilty about it. And since he desperately still wanted a relationship with them, it mattered how they would see him once the confession was public. Two, he hoped that by framing the killing as accidental, he would receive a lesser charge. And three, completely believable, he just wanted the knowledge that he'd gotten away with not telling the cops the whole truth.

Whatever Laraby's motivation was, their consensus was that they would never know.

★

STAN AND MIKE might have felt less than fully gratified by Laraby's seemingly sanitized confession, but Sandra Doorley was pleased. She prides herself on bringing killers to justice after cases have gone cold.

And she is thorough. Over the weeks after Laraby's confession, officers at the Greece PD helped sort through every piece of paperwork connected to Stephanie's case to get ready for Laraby's arraignment and trial. Stan scanned them all and burned them onto a CD—the same CD I now have. Along the way someone reread Stan and Laraby's letters, and reviewed all the relevant files, and two discoveries were made—which, in tandem, must have landed like a shotgun blast to the entire team.

The first was the line in one of Laraby's letters to Stan that had mentioned his attorney, Robert Napier: *If he knew I was talking to you, he'd have a shit fit.*

The second was the letter from Napier to David Connors, soon after Stephanie's remains were found, telling him to back off his client. Even though Napier's letter was from over a decade before, it nonetheless clearly stipulated that Laraby had invoked his right to counsel.

Without realizing it, Stan and Mike had violated Laraby's Miranda rights. Technically, Napier was still his lawyer on this matter.

The realization was earth-shattering. Laraby's confession—however inexact—was inadmissible. The indictment was null and void. Stan and Mike's years of work just to get this hollow confession—all for nothing.

"We were devastated," Stan says. "We just couldn't believe it. It was stuffed in there somewhere amidst reams and reams of paper. We were mortified."

Stan and Mike stood there in shocked silence, surrounded by all of their work, all they'd compiled, everything they'd done to hold Laraby accountable. Quietly, Captain Patrick Phelan slipped away to phone the DA's office and deliver this terrible news.

A few days later, Stan shipped off to Cuba. ADA Sandra Doorley was left to fix the mess.

41

I MUST HAVE SAID 'fuck' a million times!" Sandra says.

As soon as she learned Laraby had legal representation, Sandra called Bob Napier. When Napier realized what had transpired—that all the time Stan and Mike had spent at Great Meadow represented a violation of Laraby's right to counsel—he arranged to have his client transported to the Monroe County prison to meet with him and plan next steps. Ironically, this was what Laraby had been hoping for all along, since it allowed him to be closer to his sons. Stan and Mike had tantalized him with the transfer, saying that if he were charged with Stephanie's murder, he'd be moved for the trial. Now he'd wind up there anyway—while they got nothing on their end of the bargain.

Laraby's pain continued to worsen. He couldn't write anymore and took a few spills at Great Meadow. Something was clearly wrong, but Laraby didn't want "idiot doctors" poking around his body, so he refused to be treated.

For two weeks Napier and Laraby met regularly at the Monroe County jail. Laraby told his attorney about his life and troubles, about his mother, about how struck he was by the naïveté of people who didn't take precautions against sick people like himself.

Napier, a religious man who calls the jury system "truly mystical" but believes that the law is "not the final word on any of it," makes sure to say Laraby was a sick man with "a sexual dysfunction."

Now that the confession was no good, so was the cemetery's offer to inter Laraby when he died. What Laraby still wanted—now essentially his only desire—was to be buried off prison grounds, away from police and lawyers and correctional officers and all he despised.

But Stan and Mike had a second bite at this apple, and they let Napier know they knew well that Laraby hadn't told the truth and didn't want to. This time, they were going to make him tell it. In a way, finding that letter had been a blessing in disguise; now they had an attorney to help them secure the authentic facts.

They wouldn't negotiate anymore. They wanted Laraby to give a much fuller accounting than he'd given in the tainted confession. There was more to the story, and if they didn't get it, Laraby would rot behind DOCCS walls forever, even if that meant his taking his secrets with him.

For Napier, this was a rare case—"a win-win-win all around." Anything Laraby had ever offered was in the context of a barter, but what he wanted most—a grave—was fairly simple to attain. Napier's job was not always to have a client found not guilty, or to have a case thrown out. Sometimes it was to make sure the avenues of justice were followed according to legal and moral code.

Bob Napier is a study in contradiction. He is a man who works for murderers, sex offenders, psychopaths. The American justice system works in such a way that even the guiltiest, most abhorrent people are defended. Napier believes in this system with full faith that it is right and just. He seems to me to have an almost spiritual fealty to it, as though the system as a whole has a transcendental power greater than the sum of its human parts. He is never anything but generous and transparent with me—and it is strange to realize I am fond of this man, a man who puts himself in between terrible criminals and their prosecutors.

The ideal in this case for Napier was moral clarity, and as long as he could operate in his client's best interest, Napier couldn't imagine a better outcome than to provide closure to this case. A corroborable confession was the only thing Laraby had that anyone wanted.

Napier convinced Laraby that "things he wanted were connected to 'the real truth,'" and Laraby returned to Great Meadow, where he kept falling and his motor skills kept slipping away. Yet he was still resistant to fully cooperating. "'The DA's office isn't playing ball with me, so I'm not playing ball with them'" as Napier puts it.

As the months went on, Laraby lost all control of his hands; he began to use a pencil in his mouth to painstakingly type his letters to Napier. By December he at last had a diagnosis. He had ALS—Lou Gehrig's disease—and it would kill him.

"The insidious thing about the disease," Napier says, "is that the mind remains sharp."

Napier sensed in Laraby a strong will to live, but it didn't matter. Laraby knew what was happening. His body would betray him, and his muscles would cease to function one by one. He would lose control of his bowels and bladder, and eventually he would suffocate, unable to continue to breathe.

Right after New Year's Day in 2012, Laraby was moved to Wende Correctional Facility in Alden, New York. He was only an hour from his sons, who still refused to see him or answer his calls or letters. At Wende, Laraby was confined to the medical and hospice unit.

But still he had not given a legally admissible confession, nor one that could be corroborated; all the details he knew were public knowledge. Where before all he'd had to do was confess, now he would have to prove it was really true for the deal to move forward.

★

BY THE TIME Stan Chizuk got back from Cuba to Greece in May 2012, Laraby couldn't hold a fork to feed himself. The guards at Wende refused to hand-feed him, Stan tells me, so he'd knock over his plate and lap up his food like a dog. His hands were curled up and useless, he was in a wheelchair, and sometimes when he spoke in his now slurred and monotonous voice, his breath would catch in his throat as though he'd swallowed a glob of peanut butter. He was in constant pain. Time was running out.

In a matter of weeks, Stan Chizuk, Bob Napier, the Greece town attorney, and Douglas Meeson—the owner of the funeral home that would provide Laraby's funerary services—came to an agreement.

Laraby agreed to waive his right to remain silent and offer a complete and truthful admission—one that contained details that could be checked—in exchange for a funeral and burial off prison grounds.

On May 30, 2012, Stan, Mike, Napier, and Laraby sat around a table at Wende, and Mike hit record on his tape recorder once again.

★

MUCH LATER, WHEN I am in possession of that recording, I am tormented by it. I am afraid to hit play.

I consider Melanie, my other stepsister, who once posted on Facebook: "My sister's life is like the world inside a snow-globe: beautiful, shiny, and still. . . ."

From everything I know now about Stephanie, her life was nothing like an idyllic snow globe. Maybe Melanie needed to retreat into a safer set of circumstances.

When I emailed Melanie back in 2015, after Sandra said she'd let me listen to the recording with Melanie's blessing, I was nervous about Melanie's response. I told her I intended to travel to Rochester to start researching Stephanie's story.

Melanie had replied: "While it warms my heart that you want to keep her memory alive, there are details in that confession that I do not know myself, and do not want to know. It would be emotionally devastating to me and to my family to have that material publicized."

I'd written back and said I'd try to think of another approach.

"If this happened to you," I told my sister Vanessa as I drove up to Rochester, "I would want to know every single detail of everything you went through."

"Me, too," Vanessa said.

Then Sandra pressed the CD into my hand, even when I told her what Melanie said. "You need to hear it," she said, and there was instantly no other approach.

Everyone I talk to about Stephanie wants to know what happened to her. There are her childhood friends who ask shyly if I know what happened. There's her student Heidi, who says, "I always felt like I knew what happened; will you tell me if I'm right?"

I spent my whole adolescence with an understanding that my teacher's daughter had vanished, just dematerialized. That remained true for only a short time when she was my stepsister, erased by the phone call from my mother when I was in my last semester at Rutgers, living with three female friends, often wandering the streets of New Brunswick alone in the dark after cast parties, drunk on Jack and Gingers.

"They've found Stephanie . . ."

I remember my stepfather, quiet at my college graduation as he watched me step offstage and into my life as an adult, one month after his daughter's bones were discovered.

I think about the console table in the dining room covered in greeting cards, my dead stepsister's photo in the middle. The funeral that December, after almost eight months of the coroner holding onto Stephanie's skeleton, where I sat in the back row and listened to Melanie play the violin, watched Tom and his sisters huddle together, and then drove back to New Brunswick to wait tables at Marita's Cantina as if nothing had happened.

"This is a story that needs to be told," Sandra says.

"Her case deserved justice, and it needs to be told," Stan says.

Melanie's claim is strong, her connection to Stephanie infinitely deeper, bonded by blood. But Stephanie has been a haunting presence in my life for almost thirty years, has shaped so much of the way I view the world. I have lived in the shadow of this tragedy, too. I have experienced my own trauma—a different kind of trauma, of course—and nearly exhausted my own psychic bandwidth to come this far. Isn't this, in a way, my story, too?

I know this is true: Stephanie belongs to no one. Would she want her story told? She told her friends about her father's beatings, about the times she thrashed against the walls to get Geoff's attention, about the abortion she didn't want to have.

She told the truth when the truth wasn't easy or glamorous. She told the truth even when it humiliated her. She told the truth, even when it was hideous. She was a truth-seeker, and so, to honor her, I will be one too.

I will tell the truth though Melanie would wish it otherwise, knowing she will find it selfish, perhaps vainglorious. I wish there were some way to honor both her wishes and what I see as my duty, but there isn't. Stephanie's story calls out to be told. The only way to keep Stephanie's memory—her full, complex, vibrant memory—alive is to tell her whole story, and her death is a part of it.

42

T HE SEVENTY-MINUTE RECORDING is muffled and garbled, with a scratchy overlay, harder to decipher than the Egg McMuffin tape. On top of that, the decline in Laraby's speech is audible; it is labored, barely understandable at times. It takes me four hours to listen to it because of how often I backtrack, pressing my earbud farther into my ear, trying different combinations—listening only with one bud, switching ears, raising and lowering the volume, adjusting treble and bass. Even then, there are sentences that decrescendo to a point I can't make them out. His answers are shorter than before, and that incongruent laughter is less frequent, less hearty. Where his confession to raping Annette seems like a diversion for him, this one is decidedly more of a chore. There's no pizza or roast beef sub to relish, no backslapping quality between the men, no one-liners or ribbing.

Stan asks if he understands the implications of waiving his Miranda rights. Laraby says, "Yeah."

"Bob?" Stan says, and Napier adds, "On behalf of Mr. Laraby and in consideration of the negotiations with the town of Greece which I've reviewed with Laraby, I would consent to a waiver of his right to counsel so he is free to speak to members of the Greece Police Department."

Laraby and Napier sign a form, and Stan begins.

He tells Laraby they're there to speak about any interactions Laraby had with Stephanie with regards to her death.

"Uh, yeah, I could do that," Laraby says, "The thing I told you last year—I candy-coated it." Here, he pauses for a long breath. ". . . So the family wouldn't really know what the deal was. I just told you what you wanted to hear."

"Are you gonna tell us the full truth today? You're not gonna leave out any details in spite of how difficult it may be for somebody to learn, in the family, what the true details are?"

Laraby agrees and begins to tell the story.

The evening of July 31, 1991, Laraby says, "I was drinking my blues away, haha," and snorting cocaine. He can't remember if he was with Glen or not, but he "never needed a drug buddy."

"How much cocaine?" Mike asks.

"A lot!" Laraby answers with the most verve he can muster. He laughs a high-pitched giggle.

No one laughs with him this time.

Drunk and high, he walked to Newcastle Apartments, leaving Terry and the boys home, intending to go to the home of a woman named Karen for "a sexual encounter." When he rang the bell, Karen's boyfriend answered the door, and Laraby ran off.

He'd turned in a set of master keys when he was fired on July 26—five days earlier—but he'd made another set. "I could use [them] anytime I wanted."

He headed to Stephanie's apartment because he was "pretty sure there was no guy there." He knew the apartments surrounding hers—an old woman by herself in one, the other vacant.

"Why her?" Stan asks.

"I used to talk to her, and she was agreeable to conversation. I knew she was alone, the only thing she had was birds." Laraby pauses to remember. "A couple of birds," he says.

Laraby let himself into Stephanie's apartment. A string of bells—like Christmas bells—chimed as he opened the door. He walked through the dark and into her bedroom, where Stephanie was sleeping on her stomach, wearing only underwear. He climbed into the bed with her, and she awoke and immediately started struggling. "I told her I was much bigger and stronger, so she might as well give it up. And she did."

Laraby handcuffed Stephanie's wrists and ankles. He then picked her up and brought her to the sofa.

"Had you put anything over your face at that point?" Mike asks.

"No, but I did put something over her face," Laraby answers. "Some kind of throw thing from her couch."

At first, Laraby said, Stephanie wouldn't speak and just "stood there submissively."

He gave her a choice—please him orally or anally. "She chose oral," Laraby says. "She was so disgusted by it that I made her do it a second time. She said she'd never done it before. I teased her. I said, 'This is the first time you ever did that?'"

Then Stephanie asked him to leave. "She never screamed," Laraby says.

★

LATER, I HAVE dinner with Stan and his wife, Michelle, who's unfazed by our talk. I ask if he thinks it's true that Stephanie didn't scream. He doesn't. He believes Stephanie would have fought violently, but that no one heard her. I'm not sure. I know it's instinct to freeze sometimes in dangerous situations, to "play dead" until the threat is gone. Maybe silence was Stephanie's survival tactic.

★

STEPHANIE HAD TOLD Laraby she had a music student scheduled in the morning, and she didn't want him to be there when her student showed up.

"I didn't know what I was gonna do, but after some thought, I decided that the thing to do was eliminate the witness." The detachment both of the language—*eliminate the witness*—and the way Laraby says the words leaves me with a cold feeling inside.

He claims he never told her he was going to kill her. "She never saw it coming," he says. He approached her from behind while she was standing, put his arm around her neck, and applied pressure for several minutes. She threw up, he says, so at that point, he let her slide to the floor. "I pressed my ear against her chest to see if there were any sounds, and there were bodily sounds but no heartbeat, so I knew she was gone." Laraby strains to say this, the last word—"gone"—almost a whisper.

Mike makes sure to clarify that the killing was a conscious choice with the purpose of avoiding later identification as "the person who had contact with her."

"Yeah," Laraby says. "Because I knew her, I didn't really wanna go through with that, but . . . you know . . ."

No one speaks.

After a moment, Stan resumes. "We talked to you before about sexual assaults that have occurred . . . What made this one different where you decided you had to kill Stephanie?"

"Well, I was pretty sure that she could see my arms, which are tattooed heavily, and I knew that I was looking at probably a serious twenty-five-year sentence if it ever came up. It was just, you know, a question of survival. I wanted to take care of it and move on."

He continues. "I took the bedding—I think it was a floral print—off the bed, I lay her on the floor."

He pauses, takes several breaths. The conversation has lasted almost an hour already, and he's tiring. There's a dry clicking sound, a sort of inhaled glottal stop, like the sound of the letter K, when he breathes. Each phrase is slower as he enumerates, one by one, his actions. "I took off the handcuffs, put them in my pocket, I took off her clothes, the only clothes she wore—her underwear, and then I rolled her up in the bedding and picked her up. And uh, she was no trouble to pick up because at the time, I was bench-pressing three hundred pounds, and I had a little hundred-pound nothing to pick up, so I lay her across my shoulder, opened the door, went downstairs and out to her car, and put her in the trunk."

Mike asks where her car was parked; Laraby says there's only one place to park a car. As I listen, I remember parking outside Stephanie's apartment, likely in the same spot. I remember that as I'd stared at the nondescript building, a little brown sparrow alit on the tree branch closest to me. It chirped twice and flew off.

Stan asks what Laraby did with Stephanie's underwear. Laraby's voice becomes lighter. "I took them. I had an underwear fetish—haha. They're gone now, but I guess there's no harm in telling you that I had a foot-locker *full*, I mean *full*, of underwear that I had taken when I was a superintendent at three different complexes. Eventually, I got a delusion about having evidence and destroyed it."

Laraby explains how he trashed his collection in a dumpster by a store called Chad's. Looking for something to corroborate, Mike asks if absolutely all the souvenirs are gone.

"Oh, yeah," Laraby says dejectedly, like a kid who's dropped his ice cream cone. "Oh, it broke my heart."

"Did you take anything else from Stephanie's apartment?"

"Her purse, wallet, and checkbook." He describes the purse as brown with a strap—a precise description of the Esprit purse Stephanie brought to Charlotte Pier with Maxine and her kids. He says that's where he found her car keys, along with "the usual girly stuff, lipstick, compact, stuff like that," the keys to what he remembered as a red economy car, "maybe a Toyota or a Datsun."

He says even though her trunk was filled with "papers and books and crap," he had no problem fitting her body there because "she was so little."

The messiness of Stephanie's trunk is a detail publicly unknown. This is exactly what they need to nail the case shut for good. Real details. Details only Stephanie's actual killer would know. I ask Stan later what he thought in this moment, if he felt a little victory. "Yes," he says quickly. "Mike and I made eye contact. We knew we had him."

Laraby says that after Stephanie's body was stashed, he went upstairs to vacuum and wipe everything down with a dish towel from her kitchen, "but I was in there a million times before, documented, so I wasn't real concerned about having my prints found."

Mike and Stan ask if there was any sign that anyone heard or saw anything.

"Nobody seen me coming, nobody seen me going," Laraby says.

He's struggling to speak. "You okay?" Mike asks.

"Having a little difficulty," Laraby says quietly.

Mike pushes on. "You never returned to that apartment again?"

"Never."

"Can you take us from there?"

"I got in her car, and I drove out of the complex out to, I think it's called New Road, which leads to Ridge Road, and I turned onto Ridge Road and proceeded out to Orleans County," Laraby says.

"What was the point of driving out to Orleans County?" Mike asks.

He explains that he'd made that decision based on the terrible reputation of the county's district attorney. "The DA—he was a real screwup. He screwed up everything he touched, so I figured if it ever came to that, it would fall to him, and he'd probably screw up again." Laraby laughs for a few seconds at his own joke.

The exact location was never in the news, and sure enough, when I look on Google Maps, I see that Telegraph Road is the first left turn after the road running directly north-south that's called County Line Road.

Laraby talks about how he passed two police cruisers on the road, then a sheriff's cruiser, which shone a spotlight on his car. He panicked but held it together, and as night turned to morning, he knew he had to finish up. "It was a perilous situation; I was running out of time. The light was creeping on the horizon. So I pulled into a farmer's field and I got out, took her body out of the trunk, and carried her back to where you guys found her—or somebody found her, kids, I guess. There was a little stream. It wasn't very deep. I walked through it and came out on the other side of it into the bushes and debris and wildflowers. I took the bedding off, left her alone on her back, nude, and I took the bedding and went back to the vehicle."

"What was the point of taking the bedding with you?" Mike asks.

"I was hoping for decomposition, animals, bugs, you know the usual stuff that consumes," Laraby says.

Mike asks if he was worried about leaving anything behind, even a muddy footprint. Laraby says no, and he wouldn't have trekked mud to the car, either, since walking through the tall grass would have cleaned his shoes.

"If I recall correctly," Laraby says, "the forecast called for rain. I wasn't really concerned. I figured the rain would wash everything away when time passed."

Then he drove to a county park, where he took her checkbook out of her purse and threw the purse into a ravine. "I threw her wallet and checkbook out on the street thinking that someone would find it . . . and they'd try to cash the checks and remove the credit cards and therefore implicate themselves and that would give them somebody else to look at," he says.

"Which is kinda what happened," says Mike.

"Uh-huh," says Laraby. I can almost hear his smile.

Laraby then drove Stephanie's car to the airport and parked it in the long-term lot, where he "made a mistake" leaving the seat pushed back. This was one of the first things Tom Redmond noticed, another detail that wasn't publicly known. I imagine Stan and Mike's eyebrows rising slightly as they try to hide another thrill of vindication.

Next, Laraby walked to the Holiday Inn near the airport, hid the wrapped-up bedding outside, and went in to call a taxi. While he waited for the taxi, he chucked the car keys into the canal. He retrieved the bedding, got in the taxi, which he said was probably a Crown Vic from Town Taxi, and had the driver drop him at the Greece Ramada. He walked home from there, still carrying the bedding. He reached his house on Fielding Road at about 6:30 A.M., put the bedding in the trunk of his car, and went inside.

"Was there anyone to greet you?" asks Mike. "Was a six-thirty arrival for you kinda unique?"

"No, it happened other times, and of course, my wife was not a happy camper," Laraby says, chuckling.

"Did you get in an argument about it?" asks Mike.

"No. She was . . ." Laraby pauses. "I guess the best way to describe her after being with me for twenty years is she was kinda brainwashed."

"To this day, you haven't told anyone what happened?"

"They've got me down as antisocial, and I'm antisocial to the extreme," Laraby says. "I don't have any friends, I don't confide in people, and even my wife who I was with for twenty years, I didn't tell her."

He goes on to say that a few hours later, on August 1, he drove his car to the Ridgemont Plaza mall and dumped the bedding in the trash there. He also chucked the Newcastle keys off a footbridge near where he often went fishing.

Mike and Stan press him for more information about Glen.

(Stan later tells me that when he tracked Glen down, he was stunned to find that he was working at Newcastle again. "He's not working there anymore," Stan says.)

"I hate that kid," Laraby says. "If he was involved, I'd rat him out in a heartbeat. He's a scumbag; he ratted me out twice."

A wave of rage turns his voice dark, low, and gravelly, like an ominous thunderhead. "I would've fucking killed him years ago if it wasn't for his sister."

There are no more questions. Mike says, "I'll go ahead and stop the tape. It's twelve eleven P.M."

43

IN SUCH A story, one might expect some twist. That would be the trope in the story about the Girl Next Door. But there are no big surprises here, only lessons to learn. One is that the biggest danger to women, including trans women (and in fact, to all femme-presenting people), without a doubt, is men. Of all female homicide victims worldwide, over 50 percent are killed by intimate partners—and 98 percent of those intimate partners are men. In 2017, the FBI found that of all homicides where the victim was a woman and the perpetrator a man, and both parties could be identified, 98 percent of the killers were men the women knew in some capacity. Overall, men kill over 85 percent of all homicide victims, men or women. In 2015 in the United States, there were twenty-three recorded homicides of trans women; all but one were killed by a man.

The biggest threat to women is men, especially ones they know.

The gender theorist Judith Butler said in a 2015 interview, "Killing is an act of power, a way of re-asserting domination, even a way of saying, 'I am the one who decides who lives and dies.' So killing establishes the killer as sovereign in the moment that he kills, and that is the most toxic form that masculinity can take."

There's an undercurrent of violence constantly adjacent to women's lives. And Stephanie's life was adjacent to the life of a violent psychopath, one who was obsessed with feeling powerful, one for whom misogyny—so easily accessible in American culture—had become a

Edward Laraby, 2013

lifelong undertaking, one who was a free menace because of courtroom technicalities.

In 2009, three years before Laraby's confession, I knew him to be the man suspected of killing Stephanie and that he was behind bars. I would fantasize about driving to upstate New York, staring him in the face. I didn't know then that he had attempted to kill a guard and had gotten another twenty-five-to-life sentence. I thought then he was up for parole in 2017.

In 2015, three years after Laraby's confession, when I first heard Sandra talk about handcuffs and blankets and decomposition, I began to check and recheck the lock on my door. I began to move away from anyone in the street or on the subway who gave me the creeps.

Handcuffs on Stephanie's wrists and ankles, a blanket over her head. Her body in the creek, the rain washing her clean.

"It's almost as if he's boastful, talking about it with glee. It actually made me sick to listen to it," Sandra says. She calls it the most chilling confession she's heard in the twenty-five years of her career.

But Laraby's attorney Bob Napier tells me he swears he saw, when no one else was looking, tears in Laraby's eyes the day he confessed—"a tearfulness, an emotional release."

"Is release the same as remorse?" I ask him.

"He wanted it very clear that he didn't feel remorse," Napier says, but adds that "the desire to confess is real."

Maybe Napier means that it is human nature to shed one's stories like snakeskin, regardless of whether or not we are penitent. But maybe we make a mistake expecting someone like Laraby to act in ways we call "human."

★

KNOWING THE DETAILS is heavier and more complicated than I could have expected, but really, how could I have known what to expect? The burden of it all is like carrying a second self. Carrying all that weight feels impossible—and I think that's one reason Sandra Doorley gave me the CD. So that she is no longer in sole possession of the knowledge, the encumbrance.

Once I learn the specifics, I become the sixth person—and only the second woman—to know the truth of how Stephanie died.

★

IN THE TWO months following Laraby's confession, the Greece PD worked to corroborate it. Mike Ives charted which details were public knowledge and which were privy only to family and the police. Scuba divers went into the canal to try to recover Stephanie's car keys. Taxi drivers were interviewed to see if anyone remembered Laraby's fare from the airport to the motel.

In the end, a few facts sealed the deal: the position of Stephanie's driver seat had not been public knowledge, and Laraby admitted to "making a mistake" and leaving it pushed back. Her missing bedding was also not common knowledge. And in the photographs of Stephanie's apartment, which were never released, the leather strap with the jingle bells—which chimed as Laraby let himself in with his stolen set of keys—hangs from her doorknob.

On July 14, 2012, the *Democrat and Chronicle* reported that Laraby had confessed and was scheduled to be arraigned two days later. I posted the article to my Facebook wall. "Some solace for the Kupchynsky family," I wrote. "I only wish my stepdad had lived long enough to know that his daughter's killer had been behind bars and unable to hurt anyone else. Although I never met my stepsister, I remember when she went missing from our hometown in 1991, and I remember clearly when her remains were found in 1998, after my mother and Jerry were married, and what an outpouring of love and support filled up our house. I have always felt a strange connection to her. My stepdad would sometimes confuse us, and I always hoped that brought him some happiness."

The day of Laraby's arraignment came. By then, he was incontinent. "They had to put a diaper on him, and they made him sit there at his arraignment in a shitty diaper," Stan tells me. "He suffered. He was humiliated."

On two counts of murder, Laraby pled not guilty. This fact set me reeling at the time.

A confession does not mean a guilty plea. A plea of not guilty is standard practice. I ask Sandra if there was anything else to it. "I think he wanted a trial," she says. "I think he wanted to die with the notoriety of this."

Stan and Mike visited Wende a few more times. Now that Laraby saw that he could trade confessions for better treatment, he told them he had twelve more homicides to confess. He made other unsubstantiated claims as well. That he had once been hired to kill two Hells Angels members—he gave Stan and Mike bloody details about how he took them out on his rowboat, killed them, gutted them like fish, and dumped them overboard. When Stan and Mike looked for the men, they found them alive and well. He claimed he had killed two girls not far off from where Stephanie was found, and that he had a connection to the Double Initial murders of the 1970s—the unsolved killings of teen girls with the same first and last initials.

Stan and Mike told him they'd have to corroborate whatever he told them before offering anything in return. Laraby wrote to them, "I find your conditions unacceptable and it appears we have reached an impasse or Mexican standoff. You apparently do not trust me and I certainly have mutual feelings toward you. Here is the deal, If you want my cooperation there will be No conditions for my cooperation, And if this is unacceptable then our business is concluded. I will be content to take my secrets to the grave."

Meanwhile, he made similar promises to the Royal Canadian Mounted Police. He would share the locations of other women he'd killed if they agreed to provide a headstone after his death. He rolled them, though—his stories were never corroborated, but he got his headstone nonetheless.

In September he found his way into the spotlight again by dictating a letter to another inmate to type—to the *Democrat and Chronicle*. He said he wanted to set the story straight about himself.

> The media said that I was arraigned on murder charges, that I alledgedly confessed, that I was going to die in a couple of days, that I wanted to clear my conscience before I died, and

that through do diligence and investigative technique the Police were able to solve the case. I assumed the media would check their facts before going to press. I am some what annoyed and perhaps a little amused by this misinformation. I am what psychiatrists call a sociopath. I can assure you for better or worst that I am not burdened by morality, ethics, or remorse, and I certainly do not posses a conscience that needs to be cleansed. The Police are getting credit for solving the case and that is also incorrect. For most of my life I have been a hedonist and a opportunist I subscribe to the theory that no one gets something for nothing. with that thought in mind. When I learned that I was going to die I initiated contact offering cooperation for of value. I can assre you that I received something of equal or greater value for my cooperation. The Police did not solve anything. So as you can see someone released unverified. I thought you people were more professional.

In December Laraby tried again to reach out to Stan and Mike, shifting his tone from indignant to chummy. He'd cooked up a plan to ask to be transferred to Monroe County Jail to settle some other alleged crimes. Since that prison didn't have the appropriate medical facilities for him, he'd need a transfer to a private hospital. His deterioration was exponentially worse; by now, he could barely breathe. "If we are to resolve the multiple issues in which everyone is interested," he had another inmate write, "we should do it quickly before I am no longer able to communicate. The matter will literally become a dead issue, no pun intended."

They didn't respond.

Laraby's trial for the murder of Stephanie Kupchynsky was set to begin September 3, 2013. At a pretrial hearing in July, he mumbled from his wheelchair, his body curled, his head lolling. By September he had deteriorated to the point where he could no longer move at all. He couldn't stay in Monroe County, and it would take five men to move him back and forth every day from Wende to Rochester. His trial was postponed—indefinitely.

In early 2014 Laraby confessed from his deathbed to the 1982 ax murder of Cathleen Krauseneck in Brighton, but the details didn't line up. He got the year wrong, her hair color wrong, her positioning wrong, and he said he had sexually assaulted her; she had not been sexually assaulted.

On May 5, 2014, alone at Wende Correctional Facility, Edward Laraby took his last breath.

Bob Napier says more crimes could have been solved, more families could have had closure. Sandra says she doubts Laraby was telling the truth. Dave Connors—"the custodian of the case"—isn't sure; he says maybe Laraby killed others, but maybe he was making things up "to get out of his cell for a cup of coffee."

"Is he a guy who possibly had other victims?" Stan says. "Yeah, absolutely." But he goes on, "He struggled, and he suffered. He had to be accountable, and at the end of the day, we probably took his biggest secret, that he thought he was going to take with him, and we made him tell it."

Stan believes in justice, but he thinks it can come in varying forms. To him, the fact that Laraby's anatomy shut down around him, that a man who once thought himself so potent and unstoppable, who took satisfaction in the degradation of others, was ultimately incapacitated, feebled, and humiliated, is a retribution in its own right. The fact that Laraby was cognizant of his own demise each step of the way was a kind of a death sentence, his own body the gallows.

No one would ever know what other secrets Laraby's psychopathic mind harbored. He never faced trial for the murder of my stepsister. His indictment was dismissed two days after his death.

One year later, I drive north through sheets of pouring rain on a pilgrimage to the place Stephanie was last alive.

PART V

Burdens and Beauties

Stephanie Kupchynsky

<h1 style="text-align: center;">44</h1>

A TRUE CRIME WRITER I know once told me, when I asked about his experiences researching and presenting the intimate facts of other people's deaths, that he feels he's become part of a "community of suffering." I feel the same. But I am also grateful for the weight of all this grief, like I see reality more clearly, with less illusion.

It is difficult enough to describe or re-create people I knew well, to capture the poignancy of an entire existence and all the intricate parts of a mind. It is another thing altogether to try to evoke someone I never met. There are so many things about Stephanie I can only approximate, never capture, and all the subtle effects she had on other people, I can only repeat in their words. And even in their minds she has faded, the rich impact of her life distilled to sweet anecdotes or foreboding warnings.

So I take the voices of that multitudinous chorus and funnel them into one—my own—hoping to do justice to the significance of a single life. Still, trying to attain the elusive redemption I seek for myself and for her is like trying to catch a quick, sun-speckled fish with my bare hands.

Even for people who never knew her, she looms. Chris Weber and Justin Whipple—the boys who found her bones—are in their thirties, older now than Stephanie ever was. Justin is a chef out near Seattle, and Chris still lives in Monroe County, where he grows hops. They say that the moment they found my stepsister's bones tightened the bond between them forever; even from opposite ends of America, they still talk on the phone once a month. They are charming and sweet; our conversations have a simplicity in which I feel safe. "My dad worked for Attica as an inmate grievance supervisor," Chris tells me on the phone, "so I grew up knowing a little about the sharper edges. This was something else that reminded me of what is possible in this world."

Justin says, "It made me realize how precious life is, and someone or something can take it from you, and it's out of your control."

When Justin visits his family in his childhood home, he drives past the corner of Telegraph and Hurd Roads. "Every time I look out there, I think about it."

Chris says they felt humbled to be a part of something bigger than them. Their fortuitous find brought closure to my family; they'd done something good.

Stephanie's high school friends—the ones who tell me about my stepfather's abuse—seem permanently rattled by the loss. Lisa, a woman with a tremulous voice, who seems to me both gruff and fragile, tells me that Laraby's confession changed her entire worldview. "I always considered myself a pacifist," she says, "but he deserved to suffer."

Lisa once sat in a lecture hall in grad school, and her professor said, "Out of every one hundred people you know, one will be murdered."

She raised her hand and said, "Mine already has been."

Holly talks to me about how people's adulthoods are founded by their youth. "Stephanie's childhood set up what happened to her," she says. "It almost fit, like a Greek tragedy. How could it have a happy ending?" She says she couldn't handle hearing about Stephanie's disappearance and death at the time. She still struggles to talk about it. "The truth heals people," she says before she hangs up the phone.

Valerie, from Stephanie's Cursed Quartet in college, is still spooked by how she learned Stephanie was gone. They'd lost touch since college over some petty misunderstanding she can't remember, but in late July 1991 Valerie found herself thinking of her old friend. She got Stephanie's number from the phone book and left a message. When Stephanie didn't call back, Valerie tried again. This time, a distraught voice answered and demanded, "Why are you calling here?" It was Tom.

When the police called to tell Valerie that Stephanie was missing, she said, "I just wanted to get back in touch!"

"I was that close to talking to her," Valerie says. "When you're older, you think, 'Why did we even argue?' We could have stayed friends for years. I had a chance. I was so close."

"She was the reason I have birds," Valerie goes on sorrowfully, remembering how much Stephanie loved her pets back in West Virginia.

For all those women—for her East Brunswick friends Jane, Sharon, Janine, Michele, Lisa, and Holly; for her WVU friends Valerie and Anne; and for her friend Jessica from the New England Conservatory, who took up yoga with her as she yearned for a healthier life, all now in their fifties—the anguish is audible when they talk about her. But they talk and talk anyway, pushing past the pain, their desire to summon her for an hour outweighing the tears they might cry or the nightmares they might have.

Dave Harrison, the best friend of Stephanie's college boyfriend R. J. Vealey, talks to me for two hours while he cooks dinner for his twin boys. Dave says he blames Stephanie's killer for not only her death but, in a way, R. J.'s as well. R. J. was never quite the same after Stephanie's disappearance, Dave says. He carried a burden, a heavy sadness, which never really faded. Eight years after Stephanie went missing, just one year after her bones were found, R. J. died of a drug-related heart attack while signing autographs on tour with his new band, the Atlanta Rhythm Section, in Orlando, Florida. He was thirty-seven.

At his funeral, his widow Amy, pregnant with their third child, collapsed into Dave's arms. "Is R. J. with Stephanie now?" she asked.

"Yes, yes, he is," Dave says he told her, "and you will be, and I will be, and we will all be together in a perfect place."

R. J. was happy with his wife, Amy, and good to her, but, Dave says, "She married a broken man who was in love with a broken girl who was murdered."

For other men on the fringe of Stephanie's life, there's a sense of not having done enough—a guilty feeling they might have saved the damsel in distress, but failed. There's Phillip Brazer, from high school, who "can't let go" of Stephanie. "Why didn't I do something?" he still wonders. There's Keith Dodge, the English teacher from the Vineyard who scans my face looking for shadows of Stephanie. There's Michael

Gately, the police officer from Martha's Vineyard, who's still beating himself up over leaving Stephanie with Geoff Fletcher that night. There's Geoff himself, a man who is innocent of Stephanie's murder, but still says he feels in some way accountable.

And there are the children who loved her, who had the briefest of magical times with her. There's Heidi, who dreams of how it happened—who asks me, "I know this is crazy, but will you tell me if she was strangled?"

There's Meg, the little girl who brought Stephanie to Martha's Vineyard to begin with, her bridge to discovering the Suzuki method and the freeing self-love it encouraged.

There's Nina, who was less than ten years old when Stephanie sparked in her a love of the violin, and who remembers sitting onstage, in awe of Stephanie and Meg's duet. To Nina, Stephanie was an enchanting fairy. Flurries of Martha's Vineyard rumors found their way into the minds of those little kids. The kids on the Vineyard, Nina tells me, believed Stephanie had run off to Cape Cod. "That's as far as our minds went."

The word *disappeared*, Nina says, "goes with little kids' psyches. She was that magical. We loved her so much, and she just poofed away."

Others internalized a fear and mistrust—or at least a cynical aware-ness—of other people. Stephanie's friend Lauren from Martha's Vineyard says she's "paranoid with her kids" and "won't let them do anything."

Dave Connors says, "My daughter is in D.C., and you think, 'How many knuckleheads are right around the corner?' There is evil among us."

Bob Napier, Laraby's own lawyer, tells me, "The face value of a person should not be believed. There could be something very sinister going on. My daughters both have locks on the insides of their apart-ments—and they always use them."

When Tom Redmond's sister Molly was up for jury duty a few years ago, the attorneys asked her if she had ever known anyone who was the victim of a crime. "Yes," she answered.

"What was it?" they asked.

"Murder," she said.

"And was it solved?" they asked.

"Not exactly," she answered.

"I don't want to go to that part of my mind," she tells me, "but it's always there."

★

TOM IS HARDER to pin down than his sisters. In the early days of my research, I write him a letter, but he doesn't answer. When I learn that the violin shop he owns with his wife is right in downtown Rochester, I walk in and ask for him. But he's at lunch. Outside on the sidewalk, I see him walking with his wife. Feeling guilty for waylaying him like this, but having come this far, I say, "Tom? I'm Rachel, Stephanie's stepsister."

"Come back at four. We can talk," Tom tells me. I do.

When I return, he leads me through the front room, filled with music books, and the workshop, where the burnished glow of a hundred violins hanging on the wall casts a diffuse rosy light, and into a small office in the back.

It is hard for me to imagine the Stephanie I have come to know being with the Tom I meet. Tom is calm, measured, and devoutly Christian. Stephanie was wildfire; she might have burned him to the ground. His passion manifests in his perfectionist craftsmanship, the perfect curve of a violin's body, the perfect sheen of its finish. It's not the kind of messy passion Stephanie had. But maybe he was different then—the young man who danced the jitterbug on that June night. Maybe her murder dampened some fire he used to have that I can't see anymore. Maybe he could have tamed her. Maybe in a parallel life, she's in her fifties and driving a gaggle of their kids to church camp.

Tom and I sit in chairs facing one another as he speaks; his sadness is still palpable decades later.

He tells me the police wouldn't stop badgering him. There were police cars outside his apartment at night, and the cops grilled him for hours. Every aspect of his life was exposed.

Tom cursed himself for not invoking his right to an attorney right off the bat. They had nothing real that pointed to him, so they pressured him to confess. They invoked his religion. "You're Catholic," he tells me they said. "You know what happens to the soul."

233

For Tom and his sisters, part of the legacy of Stephanie's death is the indignant rage they carry toward the police and the justice system. "If they'd done their jobs, Stephanie would be alive," Tom says. He means that Laraby should never have been free in the first place, or that his status as a sex offender should have been known. I remind him that the Jacob Wetterling Act and Megan's Law were not enacted until 1994, three years after Stephanie was murdered; in fact, on April 30, 1998— only days after Stephanie's bones were found—Rochester congress-woman Louise Slaughter used Laraby as an example when, at a meeting of the Congress subcommittee on crime, she pushed for life in prison without parole for repeat sexual offenders.

Tom believes that, at the very least, Laraby's parole officer should have prevented him from working at an apartment complex, where he'd have such free access to victims. Tom tells me of the awful afternoon Sergeant Farrell pounded his fist on the desk, rage in his eyes, and yelled, "Where is she?" That was the incessant question that echoed in Tom's conscience—day, night, awake, asleep, alone, with others. Always. Where is she?

He tells me that one night a few months after Stephanie vanished, he came dangerously close to killing himself. He took himself out for a final meal. He ate in silence, planning to throw himself off a bridge afterward. He was so tired and beaten down. But something stopped him, some desire to survive, some flicker of hope.

Tom is married now, with two sons, working in a shop where he crafts the fine curves of stringed instruments, as gorgeous as that extrav-agant one he'd handed Stephanie, the one that had sung with the rich, sonorous strains of Bach under Stephanie's bow.

45

TWO YEARS AFTER my first trip to Rochester, in July 2017, I go back. I want to put faces to people I've only emailed or spoken to on the phone.

I take my dog and go to neighboring Charlotte, walk down the pier Stephanie and Tom walked on to the lighthouse. It is a bright July day, probably like Stephanie's last. I get ice cream at Abbott's—the last sweet thing she'd eaten—and sit on the grass under a sapphire sky wisped with clouds.

Stephanie's student Heidi and I have dinner at the Owl House. We talk about her daughter Ava, who died after only two months of life in September 2016 because she was born premature with trisomy. We talk about how some people seek truth at all costs, and some hide from it. We talk about the distance that's sometimes needed between a person and her abusive parent. We talk about loss.

She tells me she needs to know the full details of what happened to Stephanie, that she will never be at peace until she does.

So, sitting next to Heidi at the bar—two women the same age, whose lives would never have intersected if not for a woman dead over twenty-five years—I tell her the complete story of how her violin teacher, the one to whose apartment she'd had a set of keys for when she needed a break from home, was murdered. She thanks me for the truth like it was a present. It's like a weight is instantly lifted, and we begin to share stories, to laugh together. She remembers Stephanie always had a case of

Labatt Blue in her fridge. There's a new ease between us, like friends out for a ladies' night.

I email Tom to say I'll be in town and would like to meet for coffee, that we don't have to talk about Stephanie, but I'd love to say hello. He agrees to meet at eight the next morning across the highway from the new location of his violin shop. At first he seems chilly and guarded. "I need to know where you're going with all this information," he says.

I explain that I only want to be true to who Stephanie really was. We begin to tell her stories. He only knew her for three months, and I never did, yet my trove of anecdotes runs deeper. I tell him about her cursing in a Russian accent with her string quartet in college. He laughs. "I can see that," he says.

I say Jerry had a devilish sense of humor, too, and how, making Black Russians for my grad-school boyfriend, he'd exclaimed, "If I drink too many, you see me do Cossack dance!"

"That must be where she got it," Tom says. He tells me about swimming with Stephanie at Treman Park that romantic day in Ithaca. Stephanie swam into a warm spot, screwed up her face, and stage-whispered, "I think it's from one of those kids over there!"

It's the kind of joke I would make.

Tom loosens. We talk for two hours, as the conversation loops through the topics of Howard Zinn, Donald Trump, the invention of the sex offender registry, the biodiversity of the Northeast, reproductive rights, his sons, teaching, the fruitfulness of meeting a person face to face—the difference between an exchange of emails or a phone call and looking into a person's eyes, hearing their tone shift. I tell him something Heidi said the night before: "If I have learned anything, it's that everyone grieves differently."

When we speak about the decision Stephanie made to terminate her pregnancy, Tom says he thinks she made the best choice she could. She'd cried on his shoulder about it. "There are other ways to kill someone than physically," Tom says.

His eyes go soft as he remembers a day about two years after Stephanie's disappearance. He was walking down the street to work and saw a red Corolla, older and with a faded finish, like hers, he says. (I don't bother to say hers was actually a Nissan Sentra.) His memories of her are slowly changing shape. He says the Corolla had the same streaks on the windshield that Stephanie's old blades had made on hers. He halted and stared for several minutes. From behind the screen door of the house he stood outside, he heard a woman's voice call out, "Honey, come here! There's someone looking at the car!"

He was shaken back into reality. "It was kind of a wake-up call," he says. "It was so stupid, but I had such memories of special moments in that car. I had to let it go."

He invites me to see the new shop, flooded with sunlight on the second floor of a building on the outskirts of the city. It is bigger and brighter than the old shop downtown. The rooms are vast, and the violins are hung along a glass wall that looks out to the atrium of the building, so as the escalator rises, the line of polished instruments, ranging from a tiny violin for a toddler to full size, comes into focus. I can't look away. There's a sitting area with paintings, a storage room filled with cases on metal shelves, and a workshop behind a glass partition so that customers can see the craftspeople plying their delicate and precise trade. There's a sweet, woody smell, like fresh sawdust, permeating the space. Tom is proud of this shop. I am glad. Then he surprises me when he hands me a manila envelope. It's stuffed with articles and photos. "When someone's spouse dies," he asks me, "what do they do with all their stuff? I mean, how long do you hold on?"

He keeps the VHS tape where Stephanie and his sisters watched him dance the jitterbug.

The next day in Greece, I make my way to Paula's house—Paula, who would walk on the lakeside feeding the birds with Stephanie; Paula, who reminded Stephanie repeatedly that she deserved happiness. She hugs me tight as soon as I am through the door. She is a tiny woman—and I am not. I stand five inches taller and probably outweigh her by fifty pounds. My body takes up the bulk of our embrace, like I am solid and she's not. I remember the photo of her and Stephanie together, how they were the exact same size. This is as close to holding Stephanie as I will get, I think, and I prolong the embrace for a few seconds, telling myself to remember the feeling. We sit on the couch and talk for two hours while two fluffy little dogs yap in the kitchen around her silent, enormous, charcoal-colored pit mix.

"Every bird I see reminds me of her," Paula says. Then she smiles. "You see, I can't talk about it without smiling."

Like Heidi, she asks for the whole story of her friend's death. I say, "Are you sure?" She nods. I take a deep breath, and tell her. Afterward, she is quiet, absorbing it. But then, like Heidi, she's quickly back to laughing and chatting. Maybe, like me, it will take them both some time to truly process the horror.

I drive west from the city of Rochester, through suburban Greece and Brockport—where Ted Bundy once lived—out to where there are fewer and fewer houses, across the county line into Orleans County and its vast farmland. I make the first left turn. I park my car in the dirt on the corner of Hurd and Telegraph Roads. The creek is there, surrounded by trees on both sides, running under the road and continuing southwest on the other side. A woman walks down her driveway to where I stand in the bright sun, wondering if I'm in the right place. I introduce myself; she's Jill. She points up the road. "We're all related here," she says, explaining that they're all descendants of, or married into, the original Hurd family. "That's my husband's cousin's place—Roxann and Bob Taylor. If they're not home, go around back. It all happened in their backyard."

I walk up Bob and Roxann's driveway and get no answer at the door, so I tiptoe into their backyard. A brown-and-white mare trots over to investigate. As I trudge through the tall grass beyond the yard and closer to the creek, Bob appears on his back deck in wire-rimmed glasses, work-worn jeans, and a blue T-shirt that reads AMOS MOSQUITO's RESTAURANT AND BAR. I explain who I am, and he says, "I can take you out there if you like."

I follow him through rows of cornstalks, along the brush, down a steep slope to the water. I hold up the photo I have, with the numbered placards stuck in the dirt, to match the tree branches against the ones in front of me, a quarter century older. "It was right here," Bob says, and we are quiet as the stream trickles, the wind whispers, and the birds chirp.

He tells me how one morning there was a sudden throng of people on his property, and a huge excavation machine. Detectives rang their doorbell while Bob and Roxann were at work, then barged their way into the house when their fourteen-year-old daughter answered. When Bob walked out with his dog that afternoon to see what was happening, a detective bolted up the hill, calling out, "Who are you? Why are you here?"

For seven years the family had been living their lives fifty yards away from a murdered woman's body as seasons changed and nature took its course. Stephanie lay there through sunshine and snowstorms, through icy chill and sweltering heat, in daylight and in darkness.

Bob has a distinct memory of once looking out his cousin's window to see a neighbor's German shepherd running past with an enormous bone in its mouth. "Would you look at that?" his cousin said. "It must be a deer bone or something!" After Stephanie was found, Bob wondered if the bone had been hers.

Bob tells me of his younger days, when he was feistier. Migrant workers would often hang out in his fields, and he'd get his shotgun and chase them off. "There was," he says, "one night . . . where I heard loud music playing, and I thought about going out, but I was too tired and said, 'Ah, forget it.' I have always wondered, was that the night? Could I have saved her? Was she still alive out there with him? I could have shot him dead."

There it is again—a man carrying a measure of guilt for not having saved her. I smile and say, "No. No one could save her. That wasn't the night. He was here at five in the morning for only ten minutes. She was dead already. There was nothing you could have done." I see his shoulders drop in what looks like relief.

I sit with Bob and Roxann in their living room awhile. Bob talks about the miracles of beekeeping, his new passion, how all the bees' activity centers around caring for the queen. When I leave, he gives me a large jar of Bob's Bees autumn honey from his hive, made mostly from knotweed, a dark sweetness extracted from toil.

"What's your horse's name?" I ask.

"That's Justy. She's thirty," he says.

"So she was here."

"Yes, and would you believe it? My pasture used to end right near where your sister was found."

Bob, too, says "sister."

"Justy was the only witness," I say.

★

"WHAT DID YOU learn from this?" I asked Sandra in her office that rainy June day my first time in Rochester, the day my search began.

Sandra answered quickly. "No matter how safe you think you are, there are evil people out there." She said she's put a protective bubble around herself, made a conscious choice to treasure grace, not concentrate on humanity's unavoidable malevolence. "There are no chinks in my bubble. There can't be."

About Laraby, she said, "What could have stopped him? Nothing was going to stop him that night."

The trajectories of Stephanie's and her murderer's lives had inexorably led them to a cataclysmic intersection. Security, as Helen Keller once said, does not exist.

There are so many ways we try to stay solid—we eat, we make love, we dance, we fight, we remind ourselves of our bodies' substance, feeling it in the enveloping embrace of someone we love, so we can feel permanent, so we can avoid the truth of our ephemeral existence, the tiny blip we really are. So we can forget the fragility of our nature, as fleeting and escapable as a little brown-feathered sparrow on a winter tree branch.

At one point while writing this book, I had the idea of keeping their names off the same page—trying, after the fact, to separate Laraby and Stephanie, to protect her from a re-violation. But actuality interrupts every fantasy, and my responsibility is to the entire truth.

As to that, why it is my responsibility, why I'm telling the story of her life, I still can't fully say. Except that maybe the story itself is the answer. Maybe, as Rumi says, the whining of a dog for its master *is* the connection.

★

BEFORE I LEFT Sandra's office that rainy June day in 2015, she pressed something into my palm—an oval silver trinket engraved "Believe." I took it in my hands like I was receiving communion. Sandra smiled and said she takes all kinds of charms and amulets to court.

When I walked out of the building, the rain had cleared, the sun shone in a patchy sky, and the streets were more full than they'd been for two days.

It was bizarre, the buzz I had after my long day with Sandra. I still couldn't breathe deeply, harboring fresh horror in my heart, imagining what Stephanie must have felt when she realized she was going to die that night, if she ever even realized it.

Yet there was an exigent buoyancy to my mood, something fighting to float above the terror. The only thing I kept thinking was to remember to feel joy.

Out in the sunshine, my mind dwelled only on beauty: the delicate fragrance of petunias, the sun on the sand, peaches, wine, bicycles, dogs. The glimmer of moonlight on a lake. The smell of a campfire. The memory of an ex-lover's mouth.

I stood there, inhaling the scent of the earth after rain, whispering my mantra, "Feel joy, feel joy." And in an instant flare, I remembered something about Stephanie, something I'd always known but never really noticed.

Joy was her middle name.

ACKNOWLEDGMENTS

I must of course begin by expressing my boundless gratitude for my mother, Joan Kupchynsky, and my sisters, Laura Rear McLaughlin and Vanessa Warren. Their support and encouragement were the cornerstones of my confidence throughout the formidable process of creating this book and getting it into the world, and their memories are interwoven with mine in ways that only a mother's and sisters' could be.

Thanks also to my stepsister Melanie Kupchynsky, whose extraordinary love for her sister continues to inspire me.

I am inestimably obliged to Stan Chizuk, who helped me every step of the way. He fights for what is decent and right without fail, and I have grown to care for him dearly. I am thankful as well for the support of Bob Napier, who has championed this story from the beginning, for Sandra Doorley, who ignited a spark I couldn't and didn't want to extinguish, for Todd Baxter, whose strength and character have always shone through, and for Michael Gately, who was the best tour guide imaginable on Martha's Vineyard in the middle of January.

Words can not capture the appreciation I have for all of Stephanie's loved ones who spoke so openly and tenderly with me. I know it was retraumatizing for many of them to recount their memories, but they did so with magnanimity, trust, and grace.

My Lunch Bunch at school (both past and present members) kept me centered and laughing even during an entire year of remote education in a global pandemic, and their steadfast support helped me balance the writing of this book with a full-time middle school teaching career—I owe my ability to remain mostly coherent to Michelle Arniella-Cole, Sharon Maier, Kristin Mark, Giulia Saka, Joanna Santarpia, Chrissy Vissa—and especially Denise Galang and Felicia O'Hara, both writers of impressive talent who read my drafts and gave me priceless feedback. Please, readers, find and hug a teacher as soon as possible.

Thanks to these generous spirits who read my proposal or manuscript in their embryonic forms and told me what was up: Melissa Ahart, Libby Burton, Jennifer Cayer, Eve Claxton, Jonathan Dee, Heather Flaherty, Robert Kolker, Robin Messing, and Merrill Wyatt.

I am in frequent awestruck amazement by my two Daniels—my agent, Dan Conaway, at Writers House, and my editor, Daniel Loedel, at Bloomsbury. I always thought this book would be propelled into existence entirely by a contingent of women, yet Dan and Daniel proved me refreshingly wrong. They understood my book and my mission on both profound and granular levels. Dan is an unswerving, brilliant advocate who gave my book the platform and push it needed. Daniel connected with the text in a way that was perhaps kismet, and his deftness with editing is unparalleled. I would be nowhere without these two miraculous men.

Thanks also to Peggy Boulos Smith and Lauren Carsley at Writers House, and to the entire team at Bloomsbury Publishing, notably Elizabeth Ellis, Cindy Loh, Suzanne Keller, Myunghee Kwon, Grace McNamee, Nancy Miller, Miranda Ottewell, and Patti Ratchford.

And to all the friends who would always answer my little texts and inquiries along the way, who have supported this undertaking from its inception, or who helped in small but essential ways I can't fully explain: Earth Bennett, Monica Egger and Josh Abdulla, Genevieve and John Deely, Sachin Doshi, Ted Geoghegan, Dean Haycock, Emily Longo, Maureen Lundberg, Kim and Simon Mason, Jeri Merendino, Aaron Novak, Stephanie Pollicino, Nick Powers, Lexi Pritchett and John Schemitsch, Mike Robinson, Jade Rogers and Gabe Paine, Chris Schandera, Anna Schissel, John Sherrod, Amy and Eric Solomon, Lorin Taylor, Kat Vera and Mark Dahl, and Kacy Wiggum and Udi Ofer. Even if they don't know exactly how they helped, I felt their love and assistance and was buoyed.

This book is in affectionate memory of my father, Lester Rear, who died in 2013, and of my stepfather—my mom's Ukie, Jerry Kupchynsky, who died in 2009.

And it is in wild, adoring, grief-stricken memory of my heart's dad, Ed Monks, who died in 2020, and who sends me dolphins from beyond.

Above all, this book owes itself to Stephanie—whose joyous energy called to me through the veil between the living and the dead, and who will always be my true teacher.

A NOTE ON THE AUTHOR

RACHEL REAR, a New York City public school teacher and actor, holds an MA from Columbia University and an MFA from the New School. She has been published in the *Los Angeles Times*, the *Washington Post*, and numerous other publications.